ECHOES FROM A PIONEER LIFE

By
JARED MAURICE ARTER, D. D.
Harper's Ferry, W. Va.

1922:
A. B. CALDWELL PUBLISHING CO.,
ATLANTA, GEORGIA

ECHOES FROM A PIONEER LIFE

By

JARED MAURICE ARTER, D. D.
Harper's Ferry, W. Va.

1922: A. B. CALDWELL PUBLISHING CO.,
ATLANTA, GEORGIA

Copyright, 1922
JARED MAURICE ARTER

Dedicated to Mrs. Maggie Wall Arter and
Charles Oliver Arter
(mother and son)

PREPARED FOR PUBLICATION

BY

HISTORIC PULISHING

No part of this revised and edited publication may be reproduced, stored in a retrieval system, or transmitted, in any form, or by any means, electronic, mechanical, photocopying, recording, or otherwise, without the prior consent of the publisher.

All Rights Reserved.
HISTORIC PULISHING
©2017

CHAPTER I

BIRTH AND EARLY BOYHOOD

The subject of this autobiography, Jared Maurice Arter, was born a slave Jan. 27, 1850. He first saw the light in a little one-room log cabin, on a small farm lying on both sides of the Winchester Turnpike and the Shepherdstown Highway, at their crossing.

The Big House on this farm, located four miles from each, marked the halfway point between the now famous towns of Harper's Ferry and Charles Town both in Jefferson County, W. Va. Jared well remembers the John Brown Raid and the great excitement arising therefrom.

The master of the Little plantation, William Schaeffer, of Pennsylvania Dutch extraction, was inspector of arms in the United States Arsenal at Harper's Ferry. He was accustomed to rise and leave home on horseback at 5 o'clock of mornings, to eat breakfast with his mother and father in Bolivar, and to go from there to his work in the arsenal. On the morning of the John Brown Raid he left at 5 o'clock as usual. Soon the news spread that Brown and his men had made a raid through the county on the previous night, had taken into custody a number of the leading citizens, had captured Harper's Ferry and the arsenal and had barricaded himself and his men in the engine-house of the armory and was holding the captured citizens as prisoners or hostages.

ORIGINAL PLAN OF THE BUILDINGS OF WEST VIRGINIA INDUSTRIAL SCHOOL THEOLOGICAL SEMINARY AND COLLEGE

ORIGINAL PLAN OF THE BUILDINGS OF WEST VIRGINIA INDUSTRIAL SCHOOL THEOLOGICAL SEMINARY AND COLLEGE

For a brief while all sorts of rumors were afloat, and all the day long groups of men on horseback, armed with revolvers shot guns, and rifles, could be seen going towards Harper's Ferry, the scene of excitement. These accomplished nothing. Troops of two States, Virginia and Maryland, and a company of U. S. Marines were summoned and after two days succeeded in dislodging and capturing Brown and his sixteen white comrades.

The trial, conviction and hanging in Charles Town of John Brown and six of his men is familiar history.

On the day of his execution, Dec. 2, 1859, he handed this paper to one of his guards: "I, John Brown, am now quite certain that the crimes of this guilty land will never be purged away but with blood. I had, as I now think, vainly flattered myself that without very much bloodshed it might be done." Within a year and a half from the day of his death, the North and the South were at war with each other, and a Northern regiment, on its way to, the front, was singing:

"John Brown's body lies a-moldering in the grave: But his soul is marching on."

When Brown was hanged the excitement ran so high and fear was so great that his friends in the North might attempt to rescue him that few persons except strong men were permitted to witness the execution.

But Jared stood beside his mother, holding to her apron and saw hanged four of Brown's men, Cook, Coppie, Green, and Stephens. The scene all around was very war-like, but Jared at the time knew little of what it all meant. Soon the flames of a dreadful war broke forth and raged for four years.

More than once Jared saw the great Federal and Confederate armies marching along the highway, moving sometimes westward, sometimes eastward, sometimes deliberately, sometimes in hasty retreat. Twice in the course of that war, and for several weeks each time, the home of the master and slaves was between the firing lines of the two armies.

Some nerve-wrecking scenes were witnessed at these times, especially when assaults were made by first one side and then the other, or when the pickets were being relieved, or when a determined and stubborn effort was made by one army to drive the other back.

The cellars of the homes were much used at these times.

The last time that this situation occurred, in the summer of 1863, one could scarcely venture to go to the spring, woodpile or garden without being shot at.

REV. JARED M. ARTER, PH. B., D. D., PRESIDENT WEST VA. INDUSTRIAL SCHOOL, THEOLOGICAL SEMINARY AND COLLEGE, AND PRINCIPAL HILL TOP GRADED SCHOOL, FROM SEPT. 1, 1908, TO JUNE 15, 1915.

Jared knows almost nothing of his direct ancestry beyond his mother and father. His father, Jeremiah Arter, was a slave, belonging to Wm. Grove of Duffield, Jefferson Co., W. Va. He was married three times. In height he was about six feet, weighing about 200 pounds, of dark complexion, positive and stern in disposition, and could read and write a little, was quick-witted, especially good in figures, a miller by trade, having had charge, at different times, of four different mills. These were at Charles Town, Flowing Springs, Halltown, and the Bloomery, all in Jefferson County. He was much thought of by his master and by all who knew him intimately. He died at the age of 72 from paralysis, the effect of a fall down the stairway of the mill. This accident occurred in 1857, just preceding the Civil War. But like many other slaves he seems to have gotten a vision of the coming freedom. Jared's mother, Hannah Frances Stephenson Arter, was a slave, and 38 years younger than his father. She was illiterate, but quite intelligent, a devout Christian. Queenly, cultured, and refined through having grown up in the services of some of the first families of Virginia. She had a strain of Indian but a larger per cent of white blood coursing through her veins. She was thoroughly up in domestic science as acquired by practice. She was highly respected by the people of the neighborhood, white and colored, was very motherly toward all and was much respected and loved by all the children of the little plantation both white, and other colored children, as well as by her own.

She was married the second time. She and her family were freed by the Emancipation Proclamation of 1863; and in the fall of 1864 with second husband and seven children by first husband, and two children by second marriage, she moved to Washington, D. C., where she and most of the family remained about 16 years.

JARED'S MOTHER, MRS. HANNAH FRANCES STEPHENSON ARTER

CHAPTER II

JARED'S FIRST FOUR YEARS OF FREEDOM. HIS
HOME AND WORK IN A PRIVATE FAMILY

Shortly after moving to Washington, a home was found for Jared in a private family by the name of Wealch, in Georgtown, now West Washington. The head of this family, Mr. Wealch, with Mr. Herr, formed the great flouring mill firm of Wealch and Herr of Georgetown. Jared's stepfather, for a number of years, worked for this firm. In this family, Jared remained for about five months. His principal work was to make up fires, to care for the dining room and wait table and to run errands. Jared got along well most part of the time in his new line of work, was sometimes highly praised and encouraged by good words and "tips" from the head of the family and his sons; at other times it fell to his lot to be braced up sharply by severe scolding's and keen-edged chastising lectures from Mrs.

Wealch, or Mrs. Stephenson the married daughter, or from some one of the four single daughters.

There were three sons in the family, all grown up, single young men, two of whom were very stately and aristocratic. From these Jared received a number of favors, but never an unpleasant word.

Only once did Mr. Wealch speak unkindly to him, and then his words were so terrifying and his manner so menacing that Jared's rabbit blood took possession of his being and he fled for refuge to the home of his mother in Washington.

The Wealch family and his own parents tried to persuade Jared to return, but Providence ordered otherwise.

In one of the Washington papers, of that evening was seen an advertisement for a bell-boy at Dver's Hotel. Jared answered it and was turned down because of failure to stand the test of reading numbers. He returned home, took lessons that night from a brother-in-law and answered the advertisement again the next morning and secured the position.

Here Jared remained some three or four months; and while here Providence was opening the door of hope and opportunity a little wider.

Jared early showed interest in learning; his first teacher was his father; his second was his old mistress. In the spring of 1865 his mother received a somewhat flattering proposition from a business man of the State of New York to educate, train and equip with trades her two older boys, on condition they be bound out to him until twenty-one years of age.

Jared's mother decided she could not spare William, the older; neither did William care to go. But Jared, the younger, craved to go, and pleaded for the privilege. It was granted and he went.

HIS TRIP NORTH AND HOME IN NEW YORK STATE

The time of starting, as Jared recalls it, was early in the month of April. He left home cheerfully, on his trip North, under the care of a Union soldier, a captain, returning home, having been mustered out of the service at the close of the war. Heavy rainfalls and floods had done much damage to railroads and bridges of the sections through which they had to pass. This added quite a little to the time and distance of the trip. After much delay, here and there, and running over other roads to reach desired points, they arrived at Ithaca, N. Y., about 9 o'clock at night, and took the stage for Newfield, a village eight miles distant, in Tompkins County, N. Y. There they arrived about 10:30 P. M. and Jared was ushered by the Captain into his new home, a large brown, roomy two-story structure with beautiful front and back porches, and beautiful front, side and back yards decorated with trees, rose-bushes and flowers.

Mr. and Mrs. W. W. Ayers and their daughter, Mary, ten years of age, and some near relatives and friends of the family, were there to meet, greet and welcome the captain. They also gave Jared a cordial welcome and tried to make him feel at ease and as comfortable as possible in his new home and somewhat strange environments. Mr. Ayers, and Mr. Nathaniel Gillett, his brother-in-law, in partnership, ran a, grocery, clothing, and drug store in the village, and had their homes on Main Street opposite each other.

Despite the cordial welcome and the gentle and kindly manner in which Jared was broken into his new home, environments and life, for a time, a feeling of loneliness, strangeness, and embarrassment was experienced. One very trying experience growing out of this embarrassment is well remembered. Jared was taken into the Ayers home as one of the family. He was regularly seated at the table with them for his meals. For breakfast in wintertime cakes. They seldom if ever failed in this morning service of bread during the whole of Jared's stay with them.

The remainder of the breakfast service consisted of some species of breakfast food, canned or other fruits and vegetables, potatoes, eggs, steak, ham or breakfast bacon. The cakes were of quality, size and other things were graded accordingly. Three of these cakes were as many as any one of the Ayers family would eat; and they ate as frugally of the rest of the meal and seemed well satisfied. Their dinners were considerably more substantial, but their suppers were even more frugal than their morning meals. Being in Rome, Jared tried to do as Rome did, and it is natural to imitate. So Jared watched the other members of the family and for three or four days imitated them pretty closely. But Jared was growing rapidly, had a vigorous appetite, and had been used to plenty of good, strong, wholesome food, such as corn bread, fat meat, potatoes, cabbage and beans. Had he eaten to his full satisfaction of these delicate but delicious buckwheat or wheat cakes, a dozen or fifteen would not have been too many. But with slight advance in quantity of cakes from three to five or six Jared continued to imitate the Ayers family for a few days. By that time his wolfish appetite was beginning to assert itself, almost beyond control. He got up from meals almost as hungry as when he sat down. He thought of the cornbread, potatoes and cabbage he used to enjoy to the full on the old plantation and of the abundance to which he had access through serving table in the Wealch home, and as bellboy in Dyer's Hotel. But this was as a dream and only aggravated the case. He must invent some way out of this sore trial. As stated before, he had noted that the noon meal was considerably more substantial than the rest. It was about his fifth or sixth day in the home that he determined to remain in hiding till the family were through dinner. This he did and came in just as the family and some friends had finished and left the dinner table for the sitting room. Mrs. Ayers asked Jared where he had been, said she had called him several times; that he must always be present for his meals, and that now he would have to eat all alone as they were all through. Jared forced himself, violated his conscience, stretched the blanket (it was hard for he had been trained to tell the truth and had established a reputation for being truthful) got excused for absence, and - sat down to his dinner, happy in being alone. He ate out of the dishes until the contents therein approached so near the vanishing point as to disturb his nervous system. He then, finding pie, pudding, roast beef, sweet potatoes and other things left in the side dishes of those who had gone before him, cleared up these so completely that the dog and cat had to go hungry that noon. Mrs. Ayers, returning to the dining room and surveying the table, exclaimed, "Why! Jared! You must have been starving yourself! It is very evident that you have not been eating enough! There is no need of that, we want you to have plenty. Hereafter you be sure you have enough before leaving the table. With this encouragement and now feeling more at home, Jared had no further trouble with hunger.

JARED'S PRINCIPAL WORK THAT SPRING, SUMMER AND FALL

Jared's principal work that spring, summer and fall, was to assist in caring for two horses, to care for and milk one cow, to plant and care for the garden of the Ayers and Gillett families and to help around the stores. For the first few weeks Jared was a sort of curiosity in the village. So far as he knows he was the first member of the Negro race ever to make his home in that village. His movements came in for considerable notice and remarks. A few times, friends of the Ayers family with one or more of the family, stood on the back porch and watched Jared at his work in the garden or about the premises, remarking, "He seems strong, spry and active." "I bet you he is a good worker." Jared did succeed in establishing a record as a good worker. He got along well with everybody, and passed through quite a successful spring summer and fall. Sometimes he was nicknamed "Coffee," sometimes "Shade." These were given in sport and taken as a joke. It is true, there were one or two incidents of that season that roughened Jared's way somewhat.

In the third month of his stay in the village a wrestling contest occurred between a number of the boys of the village and Jared. In this line of sports Jared was at home and succeeded in throwing the champion boy athlete of the village, a youth of his own age, the best two out of three. This developed some hostility, and led to some picking at Jared, which finally terminated in a fight between Jared and a full- grown brother of the boy athlete that had been bested in the wrestling contest. In this fight Jared was out-classed and the combat was stopped. Jared had been roughly handled and though not knocked out had been decidedly worsted. Following this episode, peace between Caucasia and Africa again reigned.

In way of education Jared had been given lessons at night by Minnie Ayers, the daughter and only child of the Ayers family.

Early in December Jared entered the village graded school. The teacher was a lady, the daughter of the captain in whose charge Jared had made the trip from Washington to Newfield. She was a competent teacher and a stern disciplinarian. This was Jared's first attendance upon a regularly organized school and he had several things to learn besides book lessons. He made the third grade and continued to stand well in his classes. Nothing out of the ordinary occurred except on two or three occasions. One morning in the third week of his attendance he had a somewhat unpleasant experience. The weather was bitter cold, the benches between the desks were loose and Jared had one standing on end close to, the stove warming it. The teacher rang the bell for the pupils to take their seats. Jared remained standing at the stove warming the bench. The teacher said to Jared, "Take your seat." Jared answered, "Yes Ma'am, as soon as I can get this bench warm." Scarcely had the words escaped his lips when a large book thrown by the teacher's hand struck him between the eyes and felled him to the floor as if shot through the heart by a rifle bullet, the bench falling on him. In a dazed state he rose and in tearful voice inquired what he had done to merit such treatment. "You insolent wretch!" exclaimed the teacher, "If you can't obey instantly when I speak to you, I will knock you senseless." The lesson went home. He learned that--

>"It was not his to make reply,
>Nor to ask the reason why,
>But to do or die."

His conduct for the remainder of the term was exemplary. A few times in course of the term the teacher had Jared recite his geography lesson as an example for the rest of the class.

In the following spring Mr. Ayers sold his home and business in Newfield and purchased a farm of 80 acres, two miles from Ithaca, N. Y., lying above the head of

Cayuga Lake and along the Trumansburg Highway. Here he began the planting and development of a fruit farm.

He laid off and mapped out 30 acres of this farm to be planted with the very best species of all kinds of fruit trees, grape vines, berry bushes, and other fruit plants. He planted some ten acres the first year, and also cultivated a large crop of vegetables, especially beans. These ten acres for trees were both plowed and sub soiled. This gave Jared his first practical knowledge of what sub soiling meant. Wheat, corn, rye, oats, barley and hay were grown mainly in sufficient quantities for home use. On this farm Jared remained and worked for about two years and six months, attending school about four months each year. It is easily seen that there was plenty to do. A hired man at $25.00 per month and board was employed for eight months each year. Along with him Jared worked most of the time. Mr. Ayers, too, in part for the sake of health, worked somewhere on the place much of the time.

From the middle of November to the middle of March Jared did the chores on the place and attended the district school located two miles distant along the Trumansburg highway. The chores consisted of feeding and milking three cows, caring for about twenty head of sheep, from six to ten head of hogs, three horses, chopping wood, and at times hulling beans.

At the end of two years on this farm Jared having been persuaded that he could do better and having become very dissatisfied, was released from apprenticeship and put upon wages. The following fall, having served for wages six months, he returned to Washington, D. C.

It was in the course of these three years and six months spent by Jared in the service of Mr. W. W. Ayers that he got a fairly good start in the primary branches of English, and a good foundation laid in regular habits of work. In Washington, finding the outlook for employment poor, and having spent ten days with his mother, and other relatives, Jared left for the State and county of his birth, Jefferson County, W. Va. The corn crop that year was large, work was plentiful and wages fairly good. Jared at once, off with his coat, and went at it. He shucked corn that fall, chopped wood in the forest in the early winter, and in midwinter when the snow, with a stiff crust on it, was ten inches deep, and when no other living soul was to be seen in any of the fields around, Jared might be seen in a 30-acre field of corn, part of the time, shovel in hand, cleaning the snow from around the shocks and then shucking the corn. Twenty days service was performed in that field that winter and the compensation was $20.00 and board. In the spring, under contract, Jared cut nearly one hundred cords of wood for burning brick, and later worked on the brick yard, later still in the summer and fall of that year, after harvesting, he worked on the fine country mansion for which these brick were burned. This mansion was owned by Mr. Geo. Wm. Eichleburger, the owner of a large plantation and a prominent citizen of that part of the county. Jared found employment with the brick masons, plasterers and carpenters on this building till Christmas, when he returned to Washington, D. C. and entered a private school there, taught by a Mr. Cook.

CHAPTER III

THREE YEARS OF STRUGGLE AND UNCERTAINTY

In the following spring Jared returned to Jefferson County, W. Va., and secured service on a farm near Duffield, where he remained through harvest. From August to Christmas of the same year he worked for Mr. Wm. Raymy on the Roper farm adjoining the Geo. Wm. Eichleburger plantation. In course of that winter Jared cut some cordwood, split some rails, assisted in making shingles, and did some piddling jobs till spring, when he secured work on the farm of Mr. John Yates near Charles Town. Here he worked till July, harvested for Mr. Geo. Wm. Eichleburger, and in August he secured service at the paper mill of Mr. Eyster& Co., Halltown, Jefferson County, W. Va. Here Jared, under the eleven hour- day system worked on the yard for about three months, and was then transferred to the team service. Six teams of six mules each were kept busy every weekday hauling loose straw from distances requiring one, and often two-day trips. With these teams Jared and John Harris were sent as loaders and assistants. Often on account of bad roads, soft fields and upsets it was nine or ten o'clock at night, sometimes even as late as eleven when they got into the straw sheds, the place of unloading. But Jared was required to rise at five o'clock next morning along with others to begin the unloading that the teams might be ready by 7 o'clock to start on the next trip. There was much exposure in this work in many ways, for no day in the year was regarded as too rough or inclement for the teams and men to be out on the road. Jared remained in this service till April 1, 1873, at a salary of $1.25 per day.

Having been assured that wages in Pittsburgh were much better, on April 2, 1873, Jared, along with his brother, William, left for that city, where they obtained work at once in rolling mills at $12.00 per week and later secured positions on public work at $15.00 per week.

    Before this in the summer of 1869, Jared and his brother, William, signed a contract to buy, and made the first payment on, a good home in Bolivar, twin-town to Harper's Ferry. They at once wrote their mother in Washington, D. C., urging her to come and occupy the new home that it might furnish a home for her and a real home for all. Ten days later, while waiting to learn their mother's decision, their two sisters, Bettie and Laura, next to William

HOME PURCHASED BY JARED AND WILLIAM ARTER FOR THEIR MOTHER

and Jared in age, on a Sunday, came walking through the yard towards the kitchen of the old home plantation where Jared and William happened to be spending a few hours with the one time masters and mistresses. Their sisters informed them that their mother, with all the family and belongings, was on the Maryland side of the Potomac at Harper's Ferry, waiting to be moved into the new home, that the family and belongings had been brought from Washington to that point on a canal boat, run by their brother-in-law,

Beverly Payton. Jared and his brother, William, secured from Mr. Schaeffer the use of his team and at once hitched four horses to the large farm wagon, drove to the ferry and moved all into their new home, consisting of their mother, stepfather, three younger brothers, two sisters, and a niece. Jared and his brother William had planned and hoped to be in position to enter Storer College by the fall of 1871, but the enterprise of purchasing a home and having their mother move from Washington there to make a home for all, and their stepfather being sick with a spell that disabled him for any outdoor service for more than two years, caused nearly the whole weight of providing for the family to fall upon them. As a result they had to delay their plan of entering Storer for two years.

CHAPTER IV

LIFE AT STORER AND TEACHING IN PREPARATION FOR COLLEGE

October first, 1873, Jared and his brother William returned from Pittsburgh, Pa., made the last payment of $100.00 each on their home and entered Storer College. Here they found a fine body of students, for most part healthy, thrifty and alert, and a corps of teachers, scholarly, devout, faithful and painstaking. Among them were the founders of the school. Hon. N. C. Brackett, Ph. D., came to Harper's Ferry, W. Va., in '65 as principal and founder of Storer. He was an ordained minister of the Gospel, a fluent speaker, scholarly, and a remarkably fine teacher; had fine business qualities, and was a man of very great patience. He was the man for the place and times.

Mrs. Louise W. Brackett, wife of Dr. N. C. Brackett, came to Harper's Ferry in '65 as one of the founders and teachers of Storer.

She was scholarly and brilliant, a fine teacher and splendid disciplinarian and thorough in her work. A devout and memorable factor of inestimable worth in the history of Storer.

Mrs. Laura Brackett Lightner, sister of Dr. N. C. Brackett, came to Harper's Ferry as one of the teachers of Storer in '70. She was calm, deliberate, patient, painstaking, persevering, in every way a fine teacher. She is still with the school (1922) as Treasurer.

Rev. A. H. Morrell of Maine, came into the mission work of Shenandoah Valley in '65 and into the work at Storer as evangelist, pastor and theological teacher in '67. He was very spiritual, devout, magnetic, consecrated, whole-souled. Jared and all who came under the instruction of these faithful teachers owe them much.

Miss Annie Dudley, now Mrs. Annie Dudley Bates, came into the Christian Mission work of the Shenandoah Valley in '65, and remained for a number of years. She was a whole-souled, consecrated woman, overflowing with the evangelistic spirit. She will always be well remembered by those who sat under her influence.

DR. N. C. BRACKETT, MRS. LOUISE W. BRACKETT AND MRS. LAURA BRACKETT LIGHTNER, FOUNDERS OF STORER COLLEGE

Here soon after entering Storer Jared was asked by Mrs. L. W. Brackett to sign a temperance card on paper, which he did gladly, as he had never learned to use tobacco in any form or to drink intoxicating liquor in any form or to indulge in profanity. This act became a matter of conscience, with Jared. And not only did he keep sacredly this pledge, but there grew up in his mind a strong prejudice against these degrading habits and evil practices. Indeed he has reason to be proud, especially thankful since he is quite convinced that the moral conviction, sentiments and strength entering his life from this first positive pledge and open stand against the use of intoxicating liquors as a beverage account very largely for the very creditable part he took in a strong prohibition campaign while a student in Hilldale College, and for the campaign he helped to wage against the saloon while in the Cairo Mission, meeting every Sunday afternoon with others in the county courthouse, or elsewhere, speaking against the evils of the saloon and the liquor business, seeking abolition, and for the joy that comes into his soul at every item of news announcing the success of the temperance movement and the downfall of the saloon.

Here, too, in the fall of '73, under the lucid and powerful preaching of Rev. A. H. Morrell, Jared was led fully to accept Christ and from that until now he has been a soldier of the cross, fighting along the upward way.

After six years of hard study and diligent application, teaching primary schools a part of three years, and by studying through three summer school terms, Jared became prepared for college.

In the fall of 1879, he entered the Freshman Class of Pennsylvania State College. He was cordially received by the student body, and so far as he knows, he was the first Negro student to enter that institution. The following two years he remained out of school and taught the district school of Rippon, Jefferson County, W. Va., the same school he had taught for two school years before entering college.

In the fall of 1882, he entered the Sophomore Class of Hillsdale College, Hillsdale, Mich. Being a little short of the full requirements in Greek, he graduated, Ph. B., with the class of '85.

The next two years he taught the same district school of Rippon.

In the summer of 1887, having been licensed several years before, he was ordained to the Gospel ministry, called as pastor of the college church, and elected as a teacher in Storer College.

This position he held for four years, teaching four, sometimes five subjects in the college, and pastoring in the church.

It was in the course of Jared's pastorate at this period that the foundation of the present college church was built and the cornerstone laid. He resigned in the summer of 1891 and entered the Chicago Theological Seminary, Chicago, Ill., and graduated, B. D., with the class of '94, and matriculated in Chicago University for the summer term. Shortly after graduation he was ordained as a gospel minister of the Missionary Baptist denomination and received a call to the pastorate of two Baptist churches, one at Danville, Ill., and another about 30 miles northeast of Chicago. Having received an urgent offer to teach in the Baptist Theological Seminary at Lynchburg, Va., Jared accepted the call to serve in the seminary. This school had been projected in the early eighties by the Baptists of Virginia under the leadership of Rev. Dr. Morris, pastor of Court Street Baptist Church of Lynchburg.

Later the American Baptist Home Mission Society was asked to aid in the work. They agreed, on condition that Dr. Morris would resign from his church and devote his whole time to the school as its president, else resign from the presidency of the school and allow someone to be elected president who could devote his entire time to building up the institution. At the following State convention Prof. Gregory Hayes was elected president. He was a graduate of Oberlin College, well educated, a stirring, magnetic orator, resolute and energetic, a good money getter, and a good business manager. The school grew rapidly both in students, buildings, and other facilities under his presidency. He was president at the time Jared entered upon his work there, January 1, 1895. The president turned over to Jared for the remainder of that school year his classes in Latin, Civil Government, Physics and Rhetoric, and he took the field to raise funds, make friends, and to secure students for the school.

    Jared remained as a teacher in this school for four years and besides his regular work in the school, assisted Dr. Terrill one hour after school each day for about two years in training young men for the ministry. During the summer vacations he went on the field outside the State as financial agent for the school. He spent considerable time in the cities of Pittsburgh, Alleghany, Harrisburg, Philadelphia, Pa., and in Atlantic City, and Jersey City, N. J., and a little time in the city of New York and in other parts of the States named.

ANTHONY MEMORIAL HALL, MAIN BUILDING, STORER COLLEGE, HARPER'S FERRY, W. VA.

    He succeeded in interesting nearly all of the Colored Baptist Churches in these cities in the work of the seminary and led them to pledge and actually to give financial support to the school. Influenced by his representation and pleas for the school, the Pennsylvania Western Association adopted the seminary as the institution especially for which it would contribute financial support and to which it would send students. One church alone, in Pittsburgh (Ebenezer, Rev. W. W. Brown, pastor) at the time pledged, and fulfilled its pledge by contributing $400.00 annually to the seminary, to aid in supporting two students, and in the payment of teacher's salaries. Through Jared's representation it became the custom of the Western Association or a group of the leading churches to invite the president of the seminary to pay them a visit every year, and in this way many strong and lasting friends for the school were made.

Jared's stay and work in the seminary for most part was quite pleasant and successful. He saw a number of young men and young women graduate from the school even while he was connected with it that have made their mark in the world.

Jared resigned from the seminary in the summer of 1898, and in the spring and fall of 1899 he taught as the principal of a four-room public school in Hagerstown, Md. In the course of the fall term of this year he received a call from his old friend, Prof. G. E. Stephens to accept a position in Morgan College, Lynchburg, Va., of which Prof. Stephens was president. As he had contracted for a year, the education board of the schools of Hagerstown would not release him till the first of the year 1900. Hence on January 1, 19,00 he began teaching in Morgan College or Morgan College annex at Lynchburg. His position here was quite agreeable and his work quite enjoyable. He soon became on easy terms with the faculty and popular with

NEW LINCOLN HALL, STORER COLLEGE

the student body. However, his stay was destined to be short. About three months before going to Morgan Jared had had a long personal talk with Rev. Dr. H. M. Ford, chairman of a committee of White Free Baptists with reference to opening up a Bible School in Cairo, Ill. This school was to be for training men for the gospel ministry and for training men and women for Christian service and mission work. The committee was sincere in desire and purpose, but a way of carrying the project into effect had not yet been revealed. Many were engaged in prayer that God would so move upon the hearts of his stewards as to lead them to finance the scheme. These prayers were answered. A wealthy, devout Christian gentleman, B. C. Jordan of Maine, who was deeply interested in the welfare of the colored people, and in the work of Elder J. S. Manning, who had spent many years as a missionary among the colored people of the Cairo Mission came forward with a pledge of sufficient means to pay the salary of a man and wife to open and conduct the school. Jared, months before, had been asked to pray for the work and to expect a call. So in two weeks after Jared had entered upon his work in Morgan College he received a communication from Dr. Ford, saying that their prayers had been answered in the provision of means for opening a Bible School in the, Cairo Mission. and that of three white men and himself proposed for the work the mantle had fallen on him (Jared). Hence he was requested without fail to be in Cairo, Ill., to take prominent part in a minister's institute to be held in the first week of the following April, and to open the Bible School on Monday of the following week. Jared broke the news to President Stephens and his good wife, and both they and Jared had some regrets that they were destined to part company so soon. But as Jared was ordained to the Gospel ministry and had full-fledged theological training, the call to the Cairo Mission seemed more directly a call from God; hence his duty was plain. So in answer to the call he resigned and on the 29th of March, after a most encouraging and soul touching good-bye and farewell by the faculty and student body, Jared was taken to the station by President Stephens and he took the train for Cairo, where he arrived the next day about 9 o'clock P. M., and found the home provided for his residence during the institute.

CHAPTER V

LIFE, TEACHING AND GENERAL WORK IN THE CAIRO MISSION FIELD

Jared's first work in the Cairo Mission was in connection with the ministers' institute under the direction of Dr. Ford. The institute opened Sunday April 1, and continued till Saturday, April 7. Two other white brethren were present and assisted Dr. Ford. Jared was on the program for three specific addresses which he delivered, and assisted in general with the rest of the program. Rev. Dr. Ford in this institute gave several lectures, rich in timely instruction. His coming to the Cairo Mission was always looked forward to with very much interest.

On Monday, April 9, 1900, with an enrollment of nine licensed and ordained ministers the Cairo Bible School proper, under the official name, The J. S. Manning Bible School, opened in the lecture room of the 15th Street Free Baptist Church., Rev. N.

Ricks, pastor. Here the school was conducted until the middle of June, when it was closed for the summer. Jared went on the field for a few weeks, visiting churches and associations in the interest of the school. In July he returned to West Virginia and spent a few weeks with his family at Rippon, and again returned to Illinois and did field work for the school till the beginning of the fall term, October 1, 1900.

Early in the summer of this year Dr. Ford, as agent for the Home Mission Society, succeeded in purchasing a staunch, two-story brick structure of eight rooms as the permanent home of the school. The new home of the school stood on the corner of 21st and Walnut Streets and had an inviting, commodious yard all around it. It was in a popular part of the city and was in every way suitable for the exalted work.

Here the school in its new home on the above date, opened with an enrollment of eleven ordained ministers and licentiates and five ladies in training for Sunday School and mission work. The student body seemed all to appreciate much their new home and the special opportunities and privileges that God, through His faithful servants of the North and their friends, had provided and opened up to them. Jared, too, was much pleased and encouraged by the manifest interest and hearty, tangible response to the endeavors made for their intellectual, moral and religious betterment and that of the Cairo Mission through them. The outlook for the school at this early stage was certainly quite promising and bright.

REV. JARED M. ARTER AND MRS. EMILY CARTER ARTER (MARRIED JUNE 3, 1890), CHARLES OLIVER, ROSE ELIZABETH AND JARED MAURICE ARTER, JR.

Thus the work in the beginning of the second term of the school, moved on very delightfully. It is readily seen that the work, this early, had developed beyond the capacity of one teacher to meet all the demands. The prudential committee and friends of the school foresaw this and in their original plans provided that a man and his wife should be employed in the school from its beginning. In line with this the five rooms on the second story were neatly fitted up and furnished and about the middle of November Jared sent for his family, a wife and three children, and located them in their new home. Mrs. Arter at once took up the work as assistant in the school. Jared remained at the head of this school as principal eight years. Eight months of each year were spent in teaching and training men for the Gospel ministry and men and women for Sunday School and mission work, and two months each year were spent on the field in visiting and working in associations and conventions and yearly meetings and General Conferences for the general interest of the school and Cairo Mission.

The eight years spent in conducting the work of the J. S. Manning Bible School of the Cairo Mission are regarded by Jared in some respects as the most exalted, practical and blessed work of his life. Men and women of Free Baptist, Missionary Baptist, and

Methodist persuasion attended the school and got the benefit of the training in the English branches taught, and in theology or the plain teachings of the Bible. They got clearer views of the great essentials, and a candid and faithful setting forth of the points of difference in belief. Of course, the school emphasized the beliefs and doctrines of the Free and Missionary Baptist denominations as those, in the judgment of the school that rested clearly and firmly on the teaching and authority of the Bible or Holy Scriptures.

But there was no friction, all moved smoothly and blessedly on and the school graduated a number of classes in the course of Jared's administration, of which a number of the younger ministers have made marked success in their work as preachers, evangelists and pastors. Some of those as young men meriting special mention are Revs. Donaldson, Hodge, Dixon, Henderson, Green, Britt, Herron, Hancock and Bullock. There are others scarcely less deserving of mention.

The one serious draw-back that Jared experienced in his career there was the early breaking down of the health of his wife. When she first went to Cairo her third child, Jared Maurice Arter, Jr., was only six weeks old. Sometime in February of the next year Jared, Jr., having fallen asleep in a draught, caught a heavy cold which fell on his bowels and placed him under the care of a doctor and careful nursing for nearly four months. Mrs. Arter herself was not very well and this extra care, though she had assistance all the while, was quite a strain upon her system. With the close of school in June, she returned to her mother's home, Rippon, W. Va., where she remained till the middle of November of the following fall, at which time she returned to Cairo with her health considerably improved. For a few months after her return she assisted in the work of the school. But before the close of the school year, in the spring of 1902, her condition of health became serious again and she gave up teaching. With the close of school in June she again returned to the home of her parents in W. Va. The following November she came again to Cairo and remained about four months. Finding the climate of Cairo so decidedly against her health, in the latter part of March she left Cairo to return no more.

When it became evident her health would not permit her to teach, Jared secured the services of Prof. J. T. Lott, who proved to be an excellent teacher and remained as assistant in the school during the remainder of Jared's administration. The year 1907 proved a sad year in Jared's life. Early in January he received the sad news of the death of his brother William, who had died with pneumonia. Jared left at once for Harper's Ferry to attend the funeral and burial services. William Arter was Jared's senior by a year and six months, and was therefore the oldest child of the family except one, Mary Elizabeth Arter, who was a year and four months older than William.

William Arter was quite a remarkable man in many particulars. In education he never went beyond the normal course in Storer. As an industrial worker he was of the highest type, as a businessman he was most prompt and reliable. As a teacher he was remarkably successful. He taught the Myers Town School in Coble Town District, Jefferson Co., W. Va., for more than 32 years, and was never once late to school in all those years.

He made a practice to be at his school most always from an hour to an hour and a half before time of opening for the day. After the first four or five years he seldom, if ever, failed to have one or more pupils to finish the grade that permitted them to enter Storer. As a husband and father he was a splendid provider, a fine disciplinarian and greatly devoted to his family. As a citizen he was loyal to his country and highly respected by almost everybody who knew him.

In speaking of his life at the time of his funeral, Dr. N. C. Brackett said, "If we had two or three William Arters in every community of this country the race problem would be settled." The maiden name of his wife was Rosie Scott of Charles Town, W. Va. At the age of eighteen when first married she was modest, gentle and a most beautiful mulatto young woman. They became the parents of six children, four girls and two boys: Estella, Rossa, Aurabella, Juanita, Charles Sumner, and Jared. The first two died when about sixteen years of age, and now sleep in the cemetery in Bolivar, W. Va., with the remains of their mother and father, in whose memory there has just been erected (Aug., 1921) at the head of their graves, by the living children, a beautiful granite monument costing $220.00. The remaining four children are Charles S., Aurabella, Jared and Juanita Arter. Chas. Sumner and Juanita are both teachers in the public schools of W. Va., and Aurabella and Jared are employees of the Federal

Government in Washington, D. C., and Pittsburgh, Pa. Jared is married and has one child. They are all upright, forward looking young people of whom any father or mother might be proud. After the burial of his brother, and spending a few days with his family at Rippon, Jared returned to Cairo and pressed on with his work. Late in March, about two months after the death of his brother William, Jared received a telegram telling him that his wife was nearing death and summoning him to come at once. Again he entered upon a sad journey to Jefferson County, W. Va. He reached Rippon about 9 A. M. the next day, after leaving Cairo, and found his wife had passed away early on the night before. After fitting funeral and burial services and spending a few days with his children and the family circle, Jared again with a sad but trustful heart, returned to Cairo and took up his work. The remaining two months of this year's school were spent with much solemn reflection and deep meditation on the mysteries of life and how to make it of greatest worth., As Jared's interest in heaven was constantly on the increase, and his work was that of Bible study and training men for the Gospel ministry and men and women for Sunday School and mission work, he determined if possible to reach a higher plane of life and service, and he has reasons to believe that his efforts to live nearer the cross have been marked by success.

With the close of this school year, after spending about two weeks on the field for the school and mission, Jared returned about the middle of June to West Virginia to spend some time with his children and his wife's people, to give and receive comfort and to plan for their future. He had at this time three living children, Charles Oliver Arter, the oldest, about sixteen years of age, Rose Elizabeth Arter, about twelve, and Jared Maurice Arter, Jr., nearly seven. While Charles and Rose were both very dear children of much promise, Jared, Jr., had a number of qualities that made him a marked child of unusual promise. But sad even to mention, he was afflicted with hernia or rupture from boyhood. His mother and father had employed the treatments of specialists for years, with promise of sure cure, but all in vain.

After the death of his mother the condition of the baby boy, Jared, weighed heavily upon the mind of his father.

The boy Jared's Aunt Lizzie Carter, had been a trained nurse at Freedmen's, D. C., and was a graduate of that institution. At this time she was a trained nurse in a private hospital at Berryville, Va., under the expert control and management of Dr. Parker, who had had more than twenty years of practice and experience in the hospitals of New York City. Baby Jared's Aunt Lizzie Carter gave most interesting accounts of quite a number of children who were placed in Freedmen's and treated for hernia while she was there, and she told how every one of them was easily and safely cured. Dr. Parker also, when approached on the subject, said he had

had many children suffering from hernia put in his hands for treatment in course of his twenty years practice in the hospitals of the city of New York, and that he never had but one to come back on his hands, and that was the first one that he treated. In view of the apparent safety and certain cure gathered from these statements Jared the father of the boy, felt it to be his bounded duty to have his boy treated and cured in his childhood days. His first mind was to send him to Freedmen's. But as his Aunt Lizzie was a nurse in Dr. Parker's Hospital, and as Dr. Parker gave such convincing argument that if trusted with the case he would return him safely and soundly healed, the child was placed in Dr. Parker's hospital for treatment with all fear of malpractice or failure removed. Indeed, so completely was all fear of any ill outcome of the case removed from the father's mind that after the child had been in the hospital under treatment for three days and all seemed going well, the father took a trip to Jamestown and spent two days in attendance upon the Jamestown Tri-Centenary. On Jared's return and visit to the hospital he found his baby boy getting on seemingly as well as could be expected, but a little fretful and wanting to go home with his father. His father said nice things to him, telling him he must remain under the doctor's special care just a few days more, that if he would be good and cheerful and remain a few days longer the doctor and his aunt Lizzie were saying he could go home a new, well boy and that his father was going to get him a new suit of clothes, a new wagon, new ball and lots of other nice things. With this counsel and these promises the baby boy, Jared, was quieted and went off to sleep. While his beloved boy was thus resting, his father returned home. On the second day following this about 9 A. M., a telephone message was received summoning the father and grandmother to come at once, that little Jared was dying. His grandmother, Mrs. Amanda Carter, and his father, hitched up a horse to the buggy and drove rapidly to

Berryville, a distance of seven miles and found little Jared in a dying condition from tetanus or lock-jaw, resulting from blood poisoning. He knew his grandmother and his father and threw his arms around their necks, and a little later there came over his face a beautifully sweet smile, as he passed out of this life, and as we believe met his dear, sweet mother in the blessed land of Paradise. This blow to Jared's heart, already deeply afflicted and sore from the loss, so recently, of a favorite brother and a dear, sweet, loving wife, will never fully heal in this life. Jared remained several weeks longer with his remaining two children, Charles Oliver and Rose Elizabeth and with his wife's people in their home at Rippon, and then took his journey again for another year's work in the Cairo Mission field. He spent six weeks on the field, visiting associations, conventions, churches and yearly meetings in quest of students and to deepen the interest in the work.

On October 1, 1907, he opened the school for another year's work. The attendance this year was creditably increased above other years. Professor Lott, who had been Jared's assistant for the last three years, was of signal help in the work. The school progressed through the year in good form and closed the last week in May, with the graduation of four young men as ministers of the gospel. After spending about four weeks visiting churches, Forward Movement Clubs, Sunday Schools, and other religious bodies in the interest of the school and mission, Jared, in company with Rev. S. R. Bulloch, pastor of the First Baptist Church of Charleston, W. Va., took a trip to Niagara Falls, N. Y., where they spent several days.

While thus associated Rev, S. R. Bullock, who was at one time a student of the J. S. Manning Bible School, and at this time besides being pastor of the First Baptist Church of Charleston, was a trustee of the West Virginia Industrial School Seminary and College, mentioned to Jared the fact that the above named school at Hill Top, Fayette County, W. Va., was without a president and sought to ascertain if a call came to Jared whether he would accept or not.

Jared regarded the matter as a little pleasant pastime and so spent no serious thought about it. In the latter part iting associations and young people's meetings preparatory of August he again returned to Cairo Mission and began visto opening the Bible School for another year's work.

While engaged in this phase of his work in the Cairo Mission he received an official call from the trustees of the West Virginia Industrial School Seminary and College, asking him to accept the presidency of that institution. This led to quite an extended correspondence. All questions having been satisfactorily answered, Jared agreed to accept. Hence he offered his resignation to the trustees of the J. S. Manning Bible School to take effect in thirty days. Rev. Dr. Ford, secretary of the educational work of the

Free Baptists, called a special convention of the leading ministers and laymen of the Cairo Mission to convene in the Morning Star Free Baptist Church, Cairo, to take under consideration the resignation of Jared and the future well-being of the J. S. Manning Bible School and the Cairo Mission. The convention met at the appointed place at 9 A. M. and adjourned at 3:30 P. M.

The subjects discussed were: 1. Resolved, That the Manning Bible School is a necessity and must be maintained.

2. That we will not accept the resignation of Rev. Jared M. Arter. These resolutions were both unanimously affirmed with the exception of one vote in the negative of the second.

Concerning the second resolution as a means of inducing Jared to reconsider his action and to remain at the head of the J. S. Manning Bible School, and in the Cairo Mission work, it was agreed if he would stay to add $200.00 a year to his salary, to give his wife employment in the school if he married again, to add $500.00 more yearly to the running expenses of the school. Besides this Dr. Ford was so confident that there was no school at Hill Top, Fayette County, W. Va., worthy of the name that they became willing as a last effort to grant Jared a leave of absence for one month to go and see for himself, feeling perfectly certain he would be led to remain at the head of the J. S. Manning Bible School. Jared accepted the leave of absence and leaving the Bible School in charge of Prof. J. T. Lott, he left the last of September for Hill Top, and opened the fall term of the Seminary there, September 28, 1908, with three assistant teachers. A district school and one year high-school were affiliated with the seminary.

Jared, as principal of the graded and high school and president of the Seminary, conducted the work for a month, was fairly well pleased with it, and accepted it in good faith. He returned to Cairo, had Prof. J. T. Lott installed as principal of the J. S.

Manning Bible School, disposed of his household goods to the trustees of the Bible School, packed up his books, pictures, book-racks and shelves, shipped them to Hill Top, and returned promptly to his work there.

CHAPTER VI

JARED'S INSTALLATION AND WORK AT HILL TOP

About the middle of November an extra session of the West Virginia Baptist State Convention met in the Seminary chapel at Hill Top and formally inaugurated Jared as President of the Seminary. Rev. Dr. I. V. Bryant, president of the State convention, in his formal address, and others as well, promised hearty cooperation and expressed high hopes for the future of the Seminary.

Jared, in his address, after expressing appreciation for the honor conferred, the confidence imposed, and desire and hope of fullest cooperation, called attention to what seemed to have been the policy of the previous administration, that of allowing things to run to the bad too long before instituting repairs. He pointed out a number of examples and had it on his tongue to speak of the bad condition of the roof of the main building, but thought it not expedient to paint too dark a picture in his first public utterance. The convention made a good impression, and adjourned leaving on the whole a bright outlook for the school.

The teachers had all been freshly inspired and imbued with a deeper sense of duty and strengthened purpose to cooperate heartily in worthy endeavor for best results in their high calling; and the student body were stirred to greater pride and interest in their choice of school and in their preparation for life's work and responsibilities. All were bent on making the year's work a prime success. But how soon the clear sky can become covered with clouds! How soon our hopes can be dashed somewhat and our joy turned into mourning for a time at least!

Just about two weeks after the close of the convention, on December 2, 1908, at 10:25 A. M., while the classrooms were all filled with students and teachers hard at work, an alarm of fire was given. Jared, who had a class in Algebra in the room next the printing office, looked along the stovepipe and seeing no sign of fire hastened to the outside and looked up at the chimney, the only one to the building, and there he discovered flames extending back from the chimney along the comb of the roof about one and a half yards long and flaring upward about two feet. By this time the yard was full of students and teachers. Mr. Malone, the printer, and one of the teachers suggested that we fight the fire. But Jared said there is no use, we have no show. Get the things out of your rooms and the furniture out of the building with all possible speed! There had been no rain for weeks, everything was as dry as tinder. There was but one well on the premises, and that 159 feet deep and the water was drawn by a windlass. We had no means of reaching the roof speedily, hence there was nothing to do but to rush things out of the building with all possible speed! This was done with a will. And in the briefest time, neighbors from all around were there and worked like heroes to help save the stuff:

furniture, books, trunks, pictures, beds, bedding, clothing, and the old dining room, kitchen and laundry, which stood apart from the main building. In the incredible time of forty-five minutes the main building was in complete ruins. The old dining room, kitchen, laundry, stable and hen-house, were saved. Jared by far suffered the largest personal loss by the fire. His books, bookcases, pictures and other belongings, shipped from Cairo, fully a month before, had just arrived in time to be opened and most of them carefully arranged in two rooms, on the second floor, to be occupied by him as bedroom and study. Two large boxes of books were yet in the printing office unopened. All of these and many of those in the two rooms above were completely destroyed. This was a total loss, as the $800.00 policy protecting them in the residence at Cairo was void the moment they were removed. The loss of the school building and other school property was estimated at $12,000. Insurance on the property was $5,000.00 but there was a debt of $2,400.00 on the building, and an outstanding debt of $1,600.00. Many tears were shed, by some of the student body and at least one of the teachers as they struggled to save what they could of the property and saw the flames so rapidly reducing to ruins what had so recently been their quiet and much loved school home. Some tearfully inquired "What shall we do now?" Jared answered, "Let us rise and build better." The trustees were notified at once of the calamity. The next day a majority of them arrived on the ground, knelt around the ruins and prayed fervently to Almighty God for courage and spiritual guidance. They then arose, discussed the situation for a time, expressed serious regrets that such a sore calamity had befallen the enterprise, but declared there must be no steps backward, so they resolved in the fear of God and in the name and interest of progress to rise and rebuild.

OLD DINING ROOM OF WEST VIRGINIA INDUSTRIAL SCHOOL, SEMINARY AND COLLEGE AT HILL TOP. ONLY BUILDING SAVED FROM FIRE.

A committee on ways and means, with Jared at its head, was appointed. A meeting of the citizens of Hill Top and Red Star was called and they agreed to be responsible for raising $3,000.00 for rebuilding. The Baptist Church organization of Hill Top granted for the remainder of that year, the use of their church for conducting the school. In less than two weeks after the fire the first step toward rebuilding was made by a digging bee. This was not as well attended as we had hoped. But a few weeks later, Mr. Stanley McNorton, a thrifty business man of Glen Jean came with his teams and a force of men, who, with a number of men from Hill Top and Red Star, began the work with a will. Meanwhile Jared, as opportunity offered, set out to canvass the business white men who had made it possible for Dr. Perkins to secure a site and erect the main building that was burned and those saved from the flames. He called first of all on Mr. Samuel Dixon of McDonald, who was the president of extensive coal works at that place. Upon entering Mr. Dixon's office he was cordially received and asked, "What is your mission?" Upon learning that the trustees were fully resolved to rebuild, and were already hard at work on a larger and firmer foundation on the old site, he said, "I would never rebuild there! That low site was never a fit place for a school! Besides you have not sufficient ground there. You need land enough as your school grows to erect new buildings and to build homes for your faculty and workers." Upon this he offered a grant to the trustees for educational and religious purposes of twenty acres anywhere along the White Oak Branch of the company's railway leading from Glen Jean to Oak Hill.

Jared thanked him for the offer, but called his attention to the strong attachment of the people to Hill Top, that there they owned their homes, and that it would be no easy matter to get them to consent to rebuild the school elsewhere. Mr. Dixon then said, write and tell your trustees that Samuel Dixon says they may go anywhere along the White Oak Branch of the company's road and select a site and if we do not own it we will secure it for them and will give them fifty acres for educational and religious purposes and in addition we will grant them the privilege of buying as much more connected therewith as they may wish. Jared thanked him kindly and said he would write the trustees at once and urge them to take the first trains to Hill Top to explore for a site.

Jared then said to Mr. Dixon, the trustees will need some backing to secure the money to push the work of rebuilding. In answer Mr. Dixon said his company would make it possible for the trustees to secure in cash as much as $8,000.00.

Jared, before writing the trustees, called upon Mr. George Jones of the Jones Bros., extensive coal operators at Red Star, and who had granted to Dr. Perkins for educational and religious use the four acres which formed the site of the school property so recently reduced to ruins by fire. He told Mr. Jones of Mr. Dixon's offer and asked him if he had any counter offer to make. Mr. Jones said he had not and gave reasons. Jared then asked him what he thought of Mr. Dixon's proposition, and what advice he would give with regard to accepting it. Mr. Jones said he thought the offer was a good one, and advised us to accept it.

Jared then wrote all the trustees, telling them of Mr. Dixon's proposition and urged them to come on a day named to consider Mr. Dixon's offer. They came in full force on the day specified, and led by a guide of Mr. Dixon's selection, they made a careful canvass of all the land along the White Oak branch of the McDonald Coal Company's road as far as Oak Hill, and finally selected the site known as the "Falkner Farm." Here they had prayers and then returned to the church at Hill Top, where they formally accepted the offer, passed resolutions of thanks to the company and appointed Jared as a committee of one to see the land properly surveyed and that an outline map was made of the same. In a few days this was done and speedy preparations were being made to build a cement-house and to begin excavations for building the main school structure.

But just in this nick of time Mr. Charles Jones, the older of the Jones brothers, having returned home from a trip South in search of health, called up Jared on the telephone and requested him to call at his residence in Oak

Hill the next day, saying he wanted to talk school matters with him.

Jared called promptly the next day and found Mr. Jones alone in his sitting room. He gave Jared a cordial invitation to come in and be seated. After exchanging a few words about the weather, he said: "I have invited you here to talk school matters with you." "My brother," he said, "told me of the proposition Mr. Dixon made you, and that you had respectfully come to him at once to learn if he had any proposition which he wished to make, and that he had told you, no, he had none, and that he had even advised you to accept Mr. Dixon's offer." Continuing, he said, "My brother and I were over to Fayetteville yesterday and we thought and talked the matter over, and we have decided to make you a proposition."

Then after inquiring more particularly about the proposition made us by Mr. Dixon, he said, "We know we must make you a better proposition." So he said, "We have decided to grant and deed outright to your trustees and their successors perpetually fifty acres of ground at Hill Top in connection with and including the old original site, to grant also the privilege of purchasing other land connected therewith if desired, and to secure for the trustees a loan of $5,000.00 to aid in constructing the building." Jared was requested to convey this proposition to his trustees and to ask them to consider it. This was promptly done, and at the earliest date convenient; all the trustees again met in full forces in the Baptist Church at Hill Top.

The president, Rev. D. C. Hunter, D. D., was prompt in calling the board to order and after a proper service of Scripture reading and prayer, the two propositions, carefully written out, were taken up and discussed. That of Mr. Dixon had previously been accepted and the land surveyed. This made it important to weigh the situation very carefully. After mature thought viewing the two propositions from every angle the board unanimously, for a number of reasons, decided to cancel their acceptance of the Dixon proposition and to accept the proposition of the Jones Brothers. Again Jared was appointed as a committee of one to have the land grant of the Jones Brothers surveyed and to convey to Mr. Dixon their change of action. A few years later it became as plain as day that the Jones Brothers

BUILDING USED BY WHITE SCHOOL AT HILL TOP. TURNED OVER TO WEST VIRGINIA INDUSTRIAL SCHOOL, SEMINARY AND COLLEGE WHEN COLLEGE BUILDINGS WERE BURNED.

proposition was very providential, for the work and burden of building and running the school became so heavy that again and again at conventions and associations, the people, through reading the deed and otherwise, had to be assured that the land was theirs and that whatever they built on it would be theirs to use or dispose of in whatever way they might wish or choose. Had this not been true it is very certain that it would have been more than doubly hard to rally the people around the enterprise, and there would have been great danger that the dissatisfaction would have become so great as to have led them to have abandoned the work altogether and thus to have lost much if not all they had put there.

But in the Jones Brothers' proposition providence removed all these drawbacks.

CHAPTER VII

A MORE COMPREHENSIVE VIEW OF THE WORK

The school at Hill Top in its beginning was a private enterprise, started by Dr. Perkins, and later was taken over by the Baptists as a denominational school. In the charter secured by the Baptist trustees the school is known as the West Virginia Industrial School, Theological Seminary and College. When all the facts and circumstances pertaining to the Baptists of West Virginia and to West Virginia itself that furnish rational ground of hope for the success of a denominational enterprise such as the school above named, are carefully weighed, carefully considered, it will readily be seen that the undertaking at that time by the Baptist denomination of West Virginia to build, support, develop and conduct a good deserving school, required much resolution and courage. The churches of the State for the most part were small. A very considerable portion of the membership was from other States, especially from Virginia. These, for the most part, were greatly attached to the mother State and regarded it as their real home. They had been reared there and most of their near kin and intimate acquaintances were still there. In their minds they were in West Virginia only for a few years to make some money, as good money at that time could be made there, then they would return home and settle down. Besides, in many parts of West Virginia, especially in the coalfields, it was not possible to buy a foot of ground for a homestead, hence many who would have tied themselves to the land by purchasing homes could not, at least, around where they had a source of employment.

Many of the pastors of the West Virginia churches were also from Virginia and other States and had in large part become rather attached to the denominational enterprises of their own home States. The Baptist Theological Seminary and College at

Lynchburg, Va., under the presidency of Professor G. W. Hayes,, at this time, was looming large, and was making many strong friends outside the State. Indeed the Flat Top Association of West Virginia, if not others, had begun to contribute yearly and quite liberally to the support of that school. Many of the strong ministers

FINISHED BUILDING OF THE WEST VIRGINIA SEMINARY AND COLLEGE AND A FEW MEMBERS OF THE W. VA. BAPTIST STATE CONVENTION, AUG. 23, 1918.

and influential leaders of the State were not convinced that the Baptists needed a school in West Virginia. The public school system in West Virginia for the most part was furnishing good schools for the colored children. Besides the high and graded schools there were the Institute below Charleston, the

Bluefield Seminary and Storer College at Harper's Ferry. The time had come, too, when there was little use of going North to solicit funds for secondary schools such as the Lynchburg Seminary or the Baptist Seminary at Hill Top. The educational and home mission work at this time North among the white people was so thoroughly and completely organized that all deserving schools were listed or catalogued. Those not listed must give full proof of their merit by work done before they could be enrolled or listed and secure financial aid. Besides the educational facilities of the Southern States for Negro education were better known by those of the North, having charge of the educational and misison work than by almost any of the people having their homes right down in the South. Hence if the West Virginia Industrial School, Theological Seminary and College was to be built, supported and successfully run, it must appeal to and depend almost wholly upon the Colored Baptists of the State, and such other friends in the State as it might find and interest.

To overcome these obstacles arising from financial weakness, division of interest and sentiment, required great courage, strong resolution and wise leadership. But despite these drawbacks and discouragements the State was blessed with a goodly number of strong ministers of the Gospel, strong pastors and strong men and women in other professions and callings and among the laity. Among the Gospel ministry were such as Dr. Daniel Straton, Dr. I. V. Bryant, Dr. C. N. Harris, Dr. R. H. McCoy, Dr. J. W. Robinson, Rev. Dr. Mitchell, Dr. D. C. Hunter, Dr. H. C. Gregory, Dr. D. C. Dean, Dr. G. W. Woody, Dr. Wm. Jackson, Dr. B. R. Reed, Dr. W. H. Crawley, Dr. J. W. Page, Dr. L. A. Watkins , Dr. J. D. Coleman, Rev. Dr. Pryor, Dr. S. E. Williams, Dr. W. T. Kenney, Dr. R. D. W. Meadows, State Missionary, and others wearing the title of D. D.

Associated with these under more modest titles were a large company of strong gospel ministers, as Rev. A. D. Lewis, Rev. L. Dabney, Rev. W. W. Hicks, Rev. E. G. Holcombe, Rev. N. A. Smith, Rev P. A. Harris, Rev. H. M. C. Reed, Rev. S. A. Thurston, Rev. R. Daniels, Rev. Frank Smith, Rev. J. J. Turner, State Sunday School Missionary, and other ministers.

Among the laity were such influential worker as Prof. J. W. Scott, Prof. Byrd Prilleman, Prof. H. B. Rice, Prof. Boyd of Charleston High School, Prof. Mosse of Hinton, Prof. R. P. Sims, Principal of Bluefield Institute; Prof. H. Hatter of Bluefield Institute; Prof. Thomas Jefferson of Hill Top, Prof. Wyley of Kimball High School. And in the medical profession among others were Dr. Lawrence and Mrs. Dr. Lawrence of Montgomery, Dr. Washington and Mrs. Dr. Washington of Hill Top, Dr. Gordon of Thurmon, Dr. Callaway and Mrs. Dr. Callaway and Dr. Anderson and Mrs. Dr. Anderson of McDonald, Dr. Holley and Mrs.

Dr. Holly of Hinton. Besides these, in the same profession were those of Huntington, Charleston, Bluefield and other places, too numerous to mention.

And of those nearer the great rank and file of the people were Brother J. P. Caul, Sisters Parker, Alexander, Fannie Cobb Carter, and others of Charleston; Sisters Hodge, Wilkerson and others of Montgomery; Brothers John, James and George Monroe, Hicklin, Clemmens, McIver, Hughes, Denson, Price, Tranum, Reynals, Wilson, Penn, Oglesby, Gregory, Higginbotham and other brethren of Red Star, Hill Top,, and Prudence, and their respective and worthy companions. Also Mrs. Oglesby of long standing as teacher, and Mrs. Prof. Jefferson, and Mrs. M. A. W. Thompson, president of the Women's Baptist State Convention, all of Hill Top, F. W. Board and Stanley McNorton, and others of Glen Jean; W. P. Palmer, wife and daughter (Maybelle) Bowles and family, and others of Sun; J. McIver and wife, and A. Callaway and family of McDonald; A. P. Straughter and wife and others of Hinton-- these all merit special mention. But to mention by name all of those of the various professions and classes, in this connection, that are highly worthy would require a volume.

The persons here named and those highly deserving but not named, becoming stirred by the burning of the school property, and by the resolute determination of the trustees to rebuild and by the liberal propositions of Mr. Samuel Dixon and the Jones Brothers, especially by that of the Jones Brothers, and moved by clearer vision, and a

REV. JARED M. ARTER, INSTRUCTOR IN VIRGINIA THEOLOGICAL SEMINARY AND VOLLEGE, LYNCHBURG, VA., JAN. 1, 1895 TO SEPT. 1, 1898.

growing sense of race pride and State pride, and by a deeper sense of racial needs and duty, began to grow in interest and responsiveness and in more perfect organization for work. Thus, from almost all parts of the State they began to rally around the denominational enterprise at Hill Top.

The fifty acres donated by the Jones Brothers enabled the trustees to abandon the old, obscure site and to make choice of a location lying along the highway between Raleigh and Fayetteville, which forms one of the most beautiful and lovely school sites to be found anywhere in the State of West Virginia.

The building originally planned to be erected was in the form of a center building between two wings. The center building was to be five stories, including the basement, and the wings four stories each. But the trustees knew that was too arduous and expensive a task to be undertaken at once with any hope of success. Hence to be practical and to meet present needs they decided to undertake that year to build the west wing of the building as planned. About the middle of June, 1909, work was commenced. A foundation, 90 feet by 44 feet, was excavated and a concrete base put in, and four-story building constructed of Charleston paving brick, for most part nearly as hard as iron. The walls for the first twelve feet were eighteen inches thick, the remainder thirteen inches. The building thus erected contains twenty-eight dormitory rooms, chapel, office, kitchen, pantries, dining room and laundry. The brick-layers that constructed this building were colored, the carpenters were white, and Prof. Hamilton Hatter of Bluefield general manager. The building was put under roof by the last of November, the doors and windows closed by rough lumber, and work ceased for that year. In the spring and summer of 1910 the doors were hung, the windows put in and a part of the floors laid, and further work for want of funds was postponed indefinitely. In the interim for the housing and conducting of the school the board of education in the summer of 1909 turned over to the colored citizens of Hill Top and Red Star, the white school property. This property consisted of fair-size school grounds and a large four-room, frame building, standing along the same highway and about 150 yards west from the site of the new Baptist Seminary building.

Here Jared, as principal of the graded and high school and president of the seminary, assisted by Prof. Thomas Jefferson, Mrs. M. A. Thompson, Mrs. M. M. W. Arter, Miss Ardelle Smith and a number of student teachers, conducted the school for a number of years of his stay at Hill Top, and while the seminary building was in process of construction. During these years the standard of the high school was advanced two years, the enrollment of students raised from 90 to 125 and three promising classes were graduated. In the year 1912 the co-operative relation between county school and the seminary was dissolved and the two schools then ran independently. At the meeting of the country school board that summer Jared was reelected principal of the high school and at the meeting of the trustees he was reelected president of the seminary. This gave Jared the choice of which he would retain, as he could no longer retain both. Although he saw that the road ahead of him would be rough and perplexing, yet because more sacred and stronger in its claims, he willingly resigned from the work of the county and State and clung to that of the seminary and church.

After the doors of the new building were hung, the windows put in and a part of the floors laid in the summer of 1910, further work on the building was quite slow and uncertain. The trustees were divided in their judgment and sentiment. Some favored paying off all debts and accumulating a good-sized fund before doing more towards completing the building. Others favored going right ahead with the completion of the building as rapidly as possible. The conservative element was in the ascendancy and so the work was not vigorously pushed.

Through State Senator Wm. Johnson, who had his home in Hill Top, and to encourage the enterprise the State legislature was led at two different times to make an appropriation for the work of $2,000.00. The first appropriation was made by the legislature at its first meeting after the burning of the building, but was vetoed by the Governor. The second was made in 1913. Jared visited the Board of Control in effort to secure this appropriation. The president of the Board instructed Jared to say to his trustees that if they would go to work, push matters and finish their building so as to be ready to open their school at the time of the opening of the State schools in the following fall, that the Board of Control would guarantee to them that the $2,000.00 would be promptly paid over to, the work. The President of the Board added that this being secured would only be a beginning of what the trustees might expect.

MRS. MAGGIE WALL ARTER, WIFE OF REV. JARED M. ARTER, D. D.

The Trustee Board at that very time was in session at the First Baptist Church of Charleston. Jared politely thanked the Board of Control for their encouragement and assurance, and with light heart and quick step made his way to the meeting of the Trustee Board, feeling sure that he had news that would gladden their hearts and that would be most heartily approved by each of them.

So at the earliest opportunity Jared secured the privilege of addressing the board and of breaking to them the glorious news from the Board of Control. Imagine the disappointment, chill, and discouragement for a brief time at least of Jared's ardor, when a leading member of the Trustee Board arose after Jared had finished his remarks, and in the briefest words said: "We don't want the State's money! We will not have our school in politics! We will run our own school."

The majority of the Board sided with this view. Jared knew, however, that the sentiment of the people over the State did not endorse this view. Hence he determined to make strenuous efforts to meet the proposition of the Board of Control.

He had printed about 500 pamphlets containing the plan, character, and purpose of the organization, and plan and instructions for organizing and conducting literary societies in connection with the same, and thus he proceeded over the State and organized nearly 80 Forward Movement Clubs and Literary Societies. He took pledges of these clubs to raise certain sums of money to push the work on the building. Some clubs pledged themselves to raise $50.00, some $100.00, some $150.00, some $200.00. Having completed these organizations, Jared obtained the privilege from the operators and made a personal canvass of more than a score of coal mines, going down in some shaft mines more than 500 feet before reaching the bottom. All these mines were wired up with electricity. In some cases the wires carried as much as 500 volts. Through these mines Jared went for most part bending low, hour after hour, and from room to room, taking personal subscriptions to be paid through the office of the companies. Most times he had a guide, sometimes he had none. As he sits down at times and thinks of his adventures in these mines he can account for the fact that he never came in contact with any of the wires, or suffered serious injury in any other way only through a remarkable presence of mind, and the marvelous providence of almighty God. Once only he was knocked flat by butting his head hard against the roof of a mine, resulting in the shedding of considerable blood; and other times, quite a few, he was made to feel quite uncomfortable for brief periods by misjudging the height of roofs and striking his head pretty hard against them. But these experiences while not enjoyed at the time, only tend to make life richer, and sometimes serve at amusing reminiscences. Very few of the clubs raised and sent in any part of their pledges in time to be applied to the effort Jared was making. This was largely due to the jealousy of certain leaders who discouraged the clubs or persuaded them to turn over whatever they raised to the Association to which they belonged, and to let it go up in the regular way with the educational money to the State convention. But despite these impediments, with what money Jared was enabled to obtain through clubs and his own personal canvassing of mines he was able to purchase material and to secure the services of Deacon Pack of the First Baptist Church of Hinton and his force of plasterers and thus to have the fourteen dormitory rooms of the second floor above the basement lathed and plastered in excellent form ready for occupancy or use by the time of the opening of the State schools in the fall. But this was far from being in position to claim the, $2,000.00 appropriated by the State. Indeed, the proposition of the State Board of Control could have been met and met in good form only by the united efforts of the whole Trustee Board and the application of all educational money raised by the Baptists in the State as building fund, to pushing the work of completing the building by the specified time. This would have been a worthy effort and a worth-while achievement. But short-sightedness, jealousy, selfishness, and a division in the Trustee Board made this impossible. So far from making any efforts to open the school in the new building that fall (1914) the Trustees at the State convention, at Wheeling, voted to close the school indefinitely and to pay off all indebtedness. Of course, it goes without saying that a part of this impeding and unwise action of the board was due to a fight against Jared. And why was there a fight against Jared? It was largely because there were a number of members on the board who wanted to be president of the school. With the vote to close the school indefinitely Jared's administration as president ended, and the school remained closed for three years. Jared has this to his credit as a consolation: When he took charge of the school as its president in the fall of 1908 the trustees had four acres in a low, obscure, site, granted to them for religious and educational purposes only, with the condition if they should ever wish to come into full possession of the land they might do so by the payment of $1,500.00. Upon this land as the main building, they had a two-story frame structure containing sixteen dormitory rooms, an office, chapel, two large class-rooms and printing office, with a useless hot-air furnace beneath. This property was valued at $6,000.00. There were other buildings valued at $1,500.00 and the furniture at $1,500.00, the total valuation of all the property being $9,000.00. Upon this property there was a debt of $4,000.00.

When Jared's administration ended in the fall of 1914, the Trustees had fifty acres deeded to them and their

STORER COLLEGE CHURCH, REV. JARED M. ARTER, D. D., PASTOR, 1917

successors perpetually, outright and valued at $12,500.00, and a four-story brick structure valued at $12,500.00, with an indebtedness of about $5,000.00. In other words, when Jared took charge of the work the trustees held for the Baptists at Hill Top School property clear of debt valued at $5,000.00. When Jared's administration ended after six years' service, the trustees held for the Baptists at Hill Top School property clear of debt valued at $20,000.00. This is saying nothing of the increase of teachers employed, the advance in salaries paid and the better-trained classes graduated. In the spring of 1914 while still serving as president of the seminary Jared received a call to the pastorate of the Baptist Church of Sun, W. Va., just two miles from Hill Top. He accepted and here he found some as fine people and as faithful members as any pastor could wish to be associated with. Two successful revivals were held, a flourishing choir was formed and the church advanced to the practice of having preaching and other divine services on two Sundays in each month instead of only one, as had been the practice in all the years before. Jared's pastoral service with this people was a most enjoyable one, and when he resigned to accept a call to another field they gave him a letter of commendation expressing their appreciation of his life and character as a man and Christian minister, and of the helpful service he had been to them as individuals and as a church, in terms and sentiments so beautiful, loving and touching as to make in his heart for that people a place warm and ever green.

CHAPTER VIII

JARED'S TEACHING AT FAYETTEVILLE AND RECALL TO THE WORK AT HARPER'S FERRY

After being released from the presidency of the seminary, Jared accepted appointment as principal of the Fayetteville graded school. Here he taught and continued to serve as pastor at Sun until the fall of 1916, when he received and accepted a recall to the pastorate of the College Church at Harper's Ferry. He began his work here for the second time September 9th, and when the school opened arrangements were made with him to take charge of the Bible work of the college, and to assist Prof. H. H. Winters in superintending the boys at Lincoln Hall. These duties were quite agreeable and the work for the most part went forward in a normal way.

There is perhaps but one thing in the course of Jared's work this year that merits special mention, and that is the revival begun on the last Sunday of that year, December 31st, 1916, and continued for two weeks, closing Sunday, January 14, 1917.

Mrs. Elizabeth M. McDonald, wife of H. T. McDonald, president of Storer College, writing to the Missionary Helper concerning this revival, said: "Storer has just witnessed one of the most satisfying revivals in her history. In two weeks nearly every student out of 157 has declared himself openly for Christ. Think of what that may mean in the next thirty years. For in a school like this it is not merely a matter of saving souls, but it is saving leaders who are going out to powerfully touch for weal or woe the other souls in their community. And so when our best singers, football and baseball players, our strongest students in all departments, put themselves on the right side, it means that just so many more safe leaders are given to the colored race and to humanity. The writer has seen many revivals, but never one like this, where at a word from the leader, several would instantly respond with professions of their desire for a changed life. To a casual observer, it seemed little short of marvelous, but when one realized the personal work done each day by the pastor, Rev. J. M. Arter, and the systematic, earnest campaigning done by the Y. M. C. A., the C. E. and the Christian boys and girls for their non-Christian classmates one realizes that in these meetings faith and works were indeed going hand in hand. Too often in a school, a revival breaks up class and disorganizes routine; it was not so with us in the last few weeks. Instead there seemed a more earnest desire to show practical Christian living by a more conscientious performance of all duties by a greater carefulness on the part of the careless. Nothing more clearly told me that one of our heedless boys was sincere in his efforts than when one morning he stopped before class to carefully explain why his lessons was incompletely prepared. In all previous years he had never deigned any explanation even when it was asked for. And between teacher and student there is a greater harmony, a more human understanding and fellowship, which is one of the sweetest experiences of the teacher's life. The Christ life did not dawn for all the same way. Some were obliged to seek Him in the storm and stress of the old time, of the old-time religion accompanied by the beautiful, old-time hymn, that we so seldom hear at Storer in these latter days; to others it was a thoughtful, sober determination to work on God's side. You will be interested in one young man, a Junior. Several years ago he started his course with a smart lad among students of his own age. Circumstances forced him to leave school, but did not take from his ambition. A younger brother and sister entered Storer before he was able to return. Two years ago he returned a freshman, while his brother and sister were already in the Junior class. What would have been so galling to the spirit of a youth of less perseverance, made him only more determined to make good. And he has made good in everything he has undertaken. Therefore, when at our closing meeting he quietly announced his decision to be a Christian, we all felt his strength would be as the strength of ten. Many times during these two weeks it seemed as if the spirit of those at the North who so earnestly pray for Storer was present with us. Often the older teachers spoke of Mrs. Anne Dudley Bates and her daily prayer for the salvation of our boys and girls. To those who know the history of Storer this revival is a fresh evidence of God's answer to prayer, so often shown towards Storer. And now that our young people have been taken under the watch-care of the church and are being helped through Bible study and special Sunday afternoon meetings to adjust themselves to the regular religious duties demanded of active Christians, we are attacking our work with fresh vigor and courage." This is certainly valuable testimony to the blessed character and true success and worth of this revival. During the remainder of this school year,

Jared's work as pastor of the church and teacher of the Bible work moved along quite normally, nothing, perhaps, meriting special mention occurred. With the close of 1917 and the opening of 1918 again we ran a revival for about two weeks and were blessed with about ten converts. During the remainder of this school year nothing deserving special mention in the line of Jared's work occurred. In the fall of 1918, a large number of the male students of Storer had been drafted and were subject to be called to the colors any day, and as the girls always outnumber the boys and now it seemed the girls in the school would be more than two to one of the boys; so for the sake of economy and as a war measure, it was decided to make an important change in the dormitory homes of students. Lincoln Hall, though in the most retired part of the campus, was originally built for the boys, and when destroyed by fire some years ago it was rebuilt for the boys. It was rebuilt of stone, large gray stone, with thick, heavy walls; a gymnasium, large dining room, kitchen, pantry, storeroom, and other rooms on the basement floor. Its halls are large and airy. Its rooms are large and well lighted, with high ceilings, and large clothes-closets. Thus in every way Lincoln Hall is the most ample, roomy and attractive dormitory on the school campus. This hall, for the reasons mentioned, was given to the girls, and the boys were transferred to Myrtle Hall, now changed in name to Mosier Hall. The president of Storer had been South a part of this year (1918) visiting a number of schools, and he had observed some practices, which he decided, would be of advantage if applied in Storer.

One was to have the boys hall superintended by a man and his wife.

So Jared and his wife, Mrs. M. M. W. Arter, were asked to move into Myrtle and to take charge of the boys. They accepted the charge and superintended the boys for two years. Mrs. Arter demanded a high standard and some of the boys thought she was too exacting.

But as we never know the full worth of privilege, service or possession till we lose them, so the old boys, some that have graduated and some that are still here seem never to tire of telling her in person or through letters how much they were helped by her careful supervision and ministry to them when sick, and how much they have missed her counsel and advice since she gave up the hall. Jared liked the work and for the most part got along well with the boys. But he esteemed his strictly religious work above all else, and he came to feel that his familiar association with the boys, and his having to police them, censure them, and discipline them at times, diminished, somewhat, his influence over them as a Gospel minister. For this reason with the close of the school year, 1920, he arranged to give up the superintendence of the boys. Each of these years was closed and the new year begun with a protracted meeting participated in by pastor, members of the faculty, church, and Christian students and on each occasion new souls were brought into the kingdom, backsliders reclaimed, and the Christian body spiritually revived and strengthened.

But the visible results of the revival efforts at the close of 1919 and the beginning of 1920 were so unsatisfactory to Jared that he secured the services of a special and strong evangelist in the last week of March, and by the grace of God through his preaching and song services and the prayers of God's people some twenty souls were led to accept Christ, and four were reclaimed. All were taken under the watch-care of the Church.

During the school year of 1920 and 1921 Jared served simply as pastor of the Church and student body. In the early summer of 1921 the harmony between the church and school that had been so cordial in relation to the pastor was now becoming disturbed and discordant.

It was evident in the interest of peace, harmony and good-will, that a separation between church and pastor should take place.

As the church had been brought to a status of activity greater than ever before, was paying larger dues, and raising more money for support of pastor and support of the church-work than ever before in its history, and was receiving greater recognition as an independent body both by the school and the other churches of the community than ever before, it seemed an opportune time for the pastor to resign.

So he offered his resignation to take effect with the closing services Sunday night of October 9, 1921.

Sometime in September of this year Jared received an urgent request from Dr. C. H. Parrish, president of Simmons University, Louisville, Ky., to take charge of the ministerial department of that institution. Jared had accepted the offer and had promised, no preventing providence, to be there to begin work Monday, October 22. But on September 29, eleven days before the expiration of his services to the college church and twenty-three days before he was to enter upon his duties in Simmons University, he was suddenly, from a vigorous state of health, struck down with a most dangerous urinary attack. In twelve hours he had to have a doctor four times, and getting almost no relief he was rushed to the local hospital of Charles Town, where he remained a week.

Here he was able to obtain slight temporary relief and to learn that his condition was very serious and that nothing short of two major and very serious operations, would probably give him any permanent relief.

Jared suggested going to Freedmen's Hospital, and the attending physician advised him to go there for treatment. He accepted the advice and went to Freedmen's determined to secure the services of a specialist on urinary troubles, to learn the worst about his condition, and to do what was advised to be the safest and best thing to do. Arriving at Freedmen's Friday, October 7, he secured the services of a specialist, Dr. Milton Francis, and was examined and told his exact trouble; that he could be patched up without operations, and given temporary relief; that in this way he might be kept alive a few months, possibly a year or more, but that he would get but little comfort and would be of little service to himself or to anyone else. But that if he would submit to two operations serious in their nature and could stand them, and the doctor assured him that he could, such treatment would make him as well as he ever was and would add ten or twelve years to his life.

Jared knew he could not endure long the dreadful suffering that had brought him so near the grave in course of the last eight or ten days, and to continue such if there was a remedy, would virtually be suicide. So he determined to chance the operations. On the eleventh of October he underwent the first operation, and was confined to bed, lying only upon back and one side for five weeks.

Then the major operation was successfully performed, and for six days the suffering was so intense and persistent that twice at least it seemed that Jared must yield up the ghost and pass to his long home. At those times he had become quite willing to go and even wanted to go, if the Lord so willed.

After six days he began to improve rapidly and after nine weeks including the one spent in the local hospital he was sent home with the assurance that he would never be troubled again with the same complaint. It is said, "Every cloud has a silver lining," and that "night brings out the stars." This was verified in Jared's hospital experience. While he suffered intensely, and the brittle cord of life seemed ready to break at any moment, he was most beautifully and comfortingly remembered by his friends. The many touching letters and cards received, a strong letter from Pres. H. T. McDonald of Storer merits special mention, the constant and earnest inquiries made, and the fervent, effectual prayers sent up to the throne of heaven for his speedy recovery by the church membership and ministry of Harper's Ferry and Charles Town, by the faculty and students of Storer, and by his white neighbors and friends of Harper's Ferry and Bolivar; also by friends in many other parts of the State and out of the State, by one organization as far away as Chicago, and through gifts of money, fruit and flowers by the Y. M. C. A. and the Y. W. C. A. of Storer, and by the members and friends of the college, faculty and church, and through a number of visits and rich gifts of choice fruits and flowers by the Lovett family of Hill Top, Harper's Ferry, the many visits, cheerful talks and fervent prayers made to the throne of heaven for him by Rev. Dr. W. H. Brooks, Rev. Dr. Waldron, Rev. Willis and other Gospel ministers of Washington, D. C., and elsewhere, the frequent visits and deep interest shown by the Storer boys of Howard University, and by Mrs. Margaret Lovett Daniels and her daughter-in-law and Miss McNorton and her young lady friends, and the visits and gifts of refreshments of Mrs. Hamlin of Y. W. C. A. work, Washington, D. C., the visit and encouraging words of Miss Hands, a teacher in Washington, D. C., and the many visits, earnest prayers, cheerful words and rich gifts of flowers and fruits, and the hearty support in so many ways given Mrs. Arter, Jared's wife, by Miss Nannie Burroughs, president of the National Training School, Lincoln Heights, Washington, D. C., and by a number of her teachers and close friends, and the deep interest, and faithful attention given him by his nephew, Chas. Sumner Arter and his nieces, Aura and Juanita Arter, and, too, the skillful, faithful, successful services of the specialist, Dr. Milton Frances, and the attentive and faithful services of the internes, and the very careful, faithful and untiring services of the nurses, especially those of Miss Ovington, Miss Moore, Miss Lovett, Miss Johnson, Miss Dunston and others, and the constant inquiries and very cheerful words of the chief nurse, Miss Irving, and the unstinted attentions, kindly services and gifts of refreshments by Mrs. John Harrod, and the unique attention, strenuous efforts and unsparing denial and sacrifices of Mrs. M. M. W. Arter to minister fully to the comfort and restoration of Jared to health and happiness. All these varied acts of Christian benevolence and human kindness, all these varied acts, springing from good-will and active desire in some way and measure to minister to the temporal and eternal comfort and well-being of Jared, the prostrate sufferer, constitute in Jared's life and history a chapter of sweet-smelling savor and blessed memory, and shall ever be recalled as a source of comfort and cherished as one of the factors that contributed so very largely to the certain and rapid restoration again to the blessed condition of normal health and active service.

CHAPTER IX

A MESSAGE TO THE RACE

"Ethiopia shall soon stretch out her hands unto God."

The English term, "Ethiop" relating to "Ethiopia," or to its inhabitants, "Ethiopians," is derived from the Latin, "Aethiops," and two Greek words, signifying "burnt face, hence dark colored, black." Ethiopia primarily designates a country and Ethiopian an inhabitant of that country.

In the Bible we first meet with the word Ethiopia in Gen. 2:13. Here it is mentioned in connection with the second branch of the river that went out of Eden to water the garden and was parted into four heads.

The account there reads: "And the name of the second river is Gi-hon: The same is it that compasseth the whole land of Ethiopia." Here there was in Asia, a country by the name of Ethiopia. This, historians in general concede.

But the term Ethiopia both in the Old and New Testament, and in ancient and modern history, in nearly every instance, applies to a country in Africa, lying south of Egypt, including the present countries of Nubia, Abyssinia and parts of other territory.

But in a wider sense, both in ancient and modern history, the terms Ethiopia and Ethiopian and Kush, the Hebrew form of the same word, are all used to designate the African or Negro race. This is the general view advanced by commentators on the text, and this is the view firmly held by Jared.

"Ethiopia shall soon stretch out her hands unto God."

These words were uttered by David, a man after God's own heart, and Israel's greatest king. They contain a divine prophecy, promise and appeal. This prophecy, promise and appeal, given by the God of Abraham, through David the son of Jesse, is a divine and most comforting and inspiring message to Ethiopia, Kush, Africa, the Negro as a race, as a people. The Psalmist, under divine inspiration, has Jerusalem in his vision as a symbol of Israel's mission and God's promise to Abraham that in his seed should all the families of the earth be blessed. And as he looks down the line of the future, Jerusalem with her symbolisms, unfolds before his inspired soul, much of her strength, beauty, blessedness and glory. And as he steadfastly gazes upon the scenes transpiring before his keen and kindling vision, he beholds the birth, death, resurrection and ascension of the Messiah, and other glories of the Messianic dispensation. He beholds many nations and peoples moved and stirred by the infinite love of God, expressed in the unspeakable gift of his only son, and by the ineffable riches and fruition of the atoning sacrifice and efficacious life of Jesus, coming to the fountain of regeneration and the waters of eternal life. And as his prophetic and beatific vision deepens and brightens he beholds Ethiopia, Kush, Africa, the Negro race, becoming roused, stirred, and moved, through catching a sound of the good news and glad tidings of great joy which shall be to all people, for unto us a child is born, unto us a son is given. And peering deep into the souls of this people and perceiving their love of peace, music, joy and their emotional nature and responsiveness to light, and love, right and truth, he proclaims the glorious, hopeful, and inspiring divine message:

"Ethiopia shall soon stretch out her hands unto God."

We have here, then, "the sure word of prophecy," referring to a specific race, the African, the Negro race.

It would seem that the Psalmist had in mind what was and perhaps what is yet, a prevailing sentiment among the more favored and enlightened peoples of the world, that the Ethiopian or Negro race is a backward race, a race that is least expected to be stirred and inspired by highest considerations, and to move along highest lines, and to aim at and strive for that which is highest and best in life.

As God through the prophecy of Jonah and the vision of Peter sought to correct the erroneous ideas of Jonah, Peter and the Hebrew people concerning His attitude toward the heathen and Gentile world; so here it seems He would correct the erroneous notions or ideas of the more favored peoples concerning His attitude toward Ethiopia. As God is no respecter of persons in the matter of salvation, neither was He in the matter of creation. "For God is without variableness or shadow of turning, the same yesterday today and for ever."

"Ethiopia shall soon stretch out her hands unto God."

This prophecy was uttered about a thousand years before the beginning of the Christian era. But a thousand years in the sight of God is "but as yesterday or as a watch in the night," is but as a few hours when it is past. And we may see the dawning forth of the fulfillment of this prophecy in Matthew's words: "And as they came out they found a man of Cyrene, Simon by name; him they compelled to bear the cross." At first Jesus bore the cross alone, just as He trod the winepress alone and died alone, the just for the unjust. Then the Cross, in part or whole, was put upon Simon and he bore it after Jesus to show that man has to bear the cross, especially the followers of Jesus, as Jesus said: "Except a man take up his cross and follow me he can not be my disciple." By many commentators, Simon, being from Cyrene, which is in Africa, is supposed to have been an African of the Negro race, therefore shadowing the suffering, sorrow and heavy burdens which the race was destined to experience and bear, in part preparatory, and in part in the actual high mission, and lofty service of the Lord Jesus Christ. Again, in the Acts of the Apostles, we read: "Behold a man of Ethiopia, an eunuch of great authority, under Candace, Queen of Ethiopia, who had the charge of all her treasure, and had come to Jerusalem for to worship." Now this man was returning and sitting in his chariot reading Esaias the prophet. Then the Spirit said unto Philip, Go near and join thyself to this chariot. And Philip ran thither to him and heard him read the prophet Esaias and said, "Understandest thou what thou readest?" And he said, "How can I except some man should guide me?" And he desired Philip that he would come up and sit with him. The place of the Scripture which he read was this: He was led as a sheep to the slaughter; and like a lamb dumb before his shearer, so opened he not his mouth: In his humiliation his judgment was taken away. and who shall declare his generation? for his life is taken from the earth. And the eunuch answered Philip and said, I pray thee of whom speaketh the prophet this? of himself or of some other man? Then Philip opened his mouth and began at the same Scripture and preached unto him Jesus. And as they went on their way they came unto a certain water, and the eunuch said, "See, here is water, what doth hinder me to be baptized?" And Philip said, "If thou believeth with all thine heart thou mayest." And he answered and said, "I believe that Jesus Christ is the Son of God." And he commanded the chariot to stand still, and they went down both into the water, both Philip and the eunuch, and he baptized him. And when they were come up out of the water the Spirit of the Lord caught away Philip, that the eunuch saw him no more, and he went on his way rejoicing.

Thus this eunuch believed in Jesus, was converted, was baptized, and went on his way rejoicing, and in the judgment of most commentators on the Bible he is regarded as an African of the Negro race and as having been an important factor in the beginning of the fulfillment of the divine prophecy, promise and appeal.

"Ethiopia shall soon stretch out her hands unto God."

But it is of this prophecy, this divine message, in its relation and application to the Negro race in the United States of North America and through them, of its relation and application to the Ethiopian race in general, especially as found in Africa, that I wish to speak and to emphasize, in particular.

"Ethiopia shall soon stretch out her hands unto God."

We have here a divine prophecy, promise and appeal made concerning a specific people and the prophecy and promise are certain to be realized, but how rich and full the harvest shall be depends on how thoroughly aroused and how hearty the response and cooperation of Ethiopia shall be with the Holy Spirit and other means of grace.

It has been nearly 3,000 years since this prophecy was uttered, and more than nineteen centuries have rolled into eternity since the angel of the Lord announced one of the greatest events in the world's history, saying: "Fear not, for behold I bring you good tidings of great joy which shall be unto all people. For unto you is born this day in the city of David a Savior which is Christ the Lord."

Within these passing centuries God in His infinite wisdom, love and power, has been unfolding and fulfilling the prophecy and promise of the text in the life and history of Ethiopia.

THE EVIDENCE OF THE FULFILLMENT OF THIS PROPHECY

At this point let us consider more carefully the evidences of the fulfillment of this divine prophecy and promise concerning the religious development and progress of the Negro race.

In the course of each decade, each score of years, each century, the sun of God's truth concerning the fulfillment of this prophecy has been rising higher and higher and His glorious, inspiring light has been shining brighter and brighter, and the inescapable and binding obligations of Ethiopia, Kush, Africa, the Negro, to make hearty response, and untiring endeavor to flee from darkness and to come to the waters, the fountain of life, to Jesus Christ the Lamb of God that taketh away the sins of the world, have been growing stronger and stronger.

It is true as the poet of sacred music sings:

"God moves in a mysterious way,
His wonders to perform.
He plants His footsteps in the sea,
And rides upon the storm.

"His purposes will ripen fast,
Unfolding every hour.
The bud may have a bitter taste,
But sweet will be the flower."

These stanzas contain rich truths that enter into the evolution of the life and history of the Negro race in the United States of America and elsewhere.

The tearing of the Negro from the soil and shores of his native land and introducing him in the dark, oppressive and corruptive life of American slavery, and holding him there with increasing rigor for nearly 250 years presents a gloomy and forlorn picture: "But every cloud has a silver lining," and "night brings out the stars."

For in the course of those long centuries of thraldom, despite privation and affliction, the slave gained valuable experience and possessions. He became trained in industry and acquired an elementary knowledge of the English language and the 'Christian religion-- a world language and a world religion. He gained also a slight knowledge of trades and of business. And after being introduced into the richest and most favored country in the world in natural resources and advantages, and multiplying till he numbered about four millions, through the instrumentality of a great Civil War in which he in army and navy numbered about two hundred thousand, he had the exalted privilege of helping to save the Union and to assist in accomplishing his own emancipation from slavery and deliverance into freedom upon the soil.

"Ethiopia shall soon stretch out her hands unto God."

In fulfillment of this prophecy and promise since Emancipation, the truths therein involved have been unfolding in marvelous and very convincing proportions. Great statesmen and seers of large vision and ripe scholarship have declared the progress of the Negro race since Emancipation has no parallel in history.

Now, along what line has this advance, this progress been most marked? Without doubt or controversy it has been along the line of religion, of belief in Jesus Christ as the son of God; of repentance, regeneration, spirituality, of the elevation of moral taste and growth in moral and Christian character.

This is strictly in line with the prophetic promise of the text. This is giving obedience to the injunction of our Lord Jesus: "Seek ye first the kingdom of God and His righteousness," and claiming the promise that all necessary temporal blessings shall be added.

On good statistical authority it is recorded that the colored people of the United States, by 1902, had built twenty-nine thousand churches.

This is an average of 743 per year.

At the same rate by this year (1922) they have built forty-three thousand churches. But the money and energy expended in erecting these church edifices constitute the smaller part of the money and energy expended in accomplishing religious progress. In securing religious literature, fuel, janitor service, and in building parsonages, securing the services of pastors and evangelists, and in fostering Sunday School and mission work, more of life energy has gone.

Another phase of the Negro's strenuous endeavors and marked progress along religious lines is found in his hunger and struggles for education, especially, religious or Christian education.

Not only has he rushed with avidity into the industrial schools, seminaries and colleges established all over the Southland by his white friends of the North especially and of the South in his industrial, moral and Christian up-building, but the colored people of the country have expended millions of dollars to found, support and run industrial schools, seminaries and colleges by their own initiative and persevering efforts.

Next to the progress made in religious belief and practice, and in Christian education and provisions therefor, has been the progress made in patriotism, in loyalty to the State and country in which they have their homes and of which they are citizens.

In spite of bitter prejudice, injustice and maltreatment, whenever the country has been in danger and its welfare threatened, the Negro has always been ready and willing to volunteer his services and to play well his part.

In all the wars of the country of any note the Negro has had a part.

In the French and Indian War, and in the war with Mexico, in the Revolutionary War and in the War of 1812, in the great Civil War, in the Spanish-American War, and in the great World War, the Negro was there and played well his part.

Again, in the matter of faithfulness and loyalty in marriage and home-building as husbands and wives, fathers and mothers, the race has made very creditable and hopeful showing and progress.

When it is remembered that man's first and highest duty is to God, his second to his country, and his third to his home, and the fact is carefully noted that the greatest strides and progress of the race have been along the lofty plains of these divine institutions, and in the God appoint order, it must, to all thoughtful persons be plain and convincing that the divine prophecy of David is being beautifully fulfilled, and that the foundation that is thus being laid in the character, life and history of the race, furnish substantial grounds for firm belief and bright hopes for the future of the race.

But this progress and promising history are largely the work and result of burnt children, of those who have passed through the furnace of affliction, privation and suffering and of their immediate children, born early enough to get vivid and burning lessons concerning the sufferings and trying ordeals of their fathers and mothers.

In their afflictions the fathers and mothers gained some knowledge of the God of Israel, that he is a God of loving kindness and tender mercies and that He pitieth them that fear Him as a father pitieth his children, and is a friend to the poor and needy. They had learned to pray and spent much time in earnest, fervent prayer to Almighty God for liberty and light. And when, through the intervention of God, the chains of slavery were broken and they were ushered into freedom and the doors of opportunity swung open, divine impulse, necessity, novelty and strong desire and wise counsel led them promptly to reach out and take firm hold upon the means at hand and to move forward in the way of religious, educational, patriotic, material and economic progress, and thus to remove themselves as rapidly and as far as possible from the old life of ignorance, privation, suffering and want.

"Ethiopia shall soon stretch out her hands unto God."

The fathers and mothers and their immediate children have laid the foundation well and made commendable and hopeful progress.

But what about their children, What about the present generation? Do they give bright promise? and will they make good? The outlook for man in this world for doing his best and making most of himself, was never brighter. We must give God the glory for this bright and splendid outlook. God's claims upon the race and upon mankind for faithful service were never stronger than they are today.

Statesmen, seers and men in every legitimate line of business are coming more and more to see and believe that the lofty principles of the Bible, the divine principles enunciated and taught by our Lord Jesus are the only principles that will solve justly and rightly and truly the many real and trying problems of this life in their relation to time and eternity.

The true Christian and faithful follower of the Lord Jesus must believe this with all his heart, soul, mind and strength. Only thus can he be what he should be. Only thus can he discharge his full duty to himself, to his fellowman and his God.

The truth here expressed is one that should be pondered much, held exceedingly dear, and sought by untiring endeavor by

Ethiopia, by Africa, in America to make it a genuine reality in her purpose and life.

"Ethiopia shall soon stretch out her hands unto God."

Ethiopia, Africa in America, the Negro, is now in the blazing light and stirring and impelling force of the fulfillment of this divine prophecy, promise and appeal. Hence it stands today as a divine command to the race, to Ethiopia, to Africa, saying, "Ethiopia, race of Africa, stretch forth your hands with mighty energy unto God, your creator and preserver and only hope for time and eternity."

The momentous question is: "Will Ethiopia, will the Negro as a race, as a people, respond and obey this divine prophecy, promise, appeal, this injunction? What is essential to insure obedience?

"Seek ye the Lord while He may be found, call ye upon Him while He is near." "Today is the day of salvation."

"Let the wicked forsake his way and the unrighteous man his thoughts, and let him return unto the Lord, and He will have mercy upon him and to our God, for He will abundantly pardon." The truths here revealed should be profoundly cherished and faithfully practiced.

There is much in the history of the African race in this country that is analogous to certain phases of the history of Israel.

Israel suffered slavery and oppression in Egypt and the Negro race suffered slavery and oppression in America. God delivered Israel from Egyptian slavery with a strong hand and outstretched arm, and he appealed again and again to this dark history and to the gratitude and loyalty due to this gracious and marvelous deliverance, as an incentive and motive to arouse, stir, persuade and impel them to loyal devotion and to forward and faithful movement along the lines of truth and righteousness.

And so, in the deliverance of the Colored race, the African race, from American slavery, the strong hand of God and His outstretched arm of providence were mighty in their workings, and strikingly visible. And through reason and conscience and the strength of analogy and through the bountiful benevolence and missionary spirit that prompted generous hearts of the North to pour out their millions and to send hundreds of missionaries all over the Southland to teach and to aid in building churches, schools and colleges for the education, Christianizing and uplift of the race, and the divine providence as well, which prompted the Caucasian race of the Southland to rise above prejudice and to open up and support a system of State schools for the education, uplift and betterment of the condition of the race in all of these direct and overruling divine and human providences, the mighty voice and power of God is heard and felt.

Yes, verily, God has been, and is, and will continue to appeal to Ethiopia, to the Negro race in America through the sense of fear arising from the dark history of more than two hundred years of cruel slavery, and through the sense of profound gratitude, loyalty and faithful service due to the gracious and marvelous deliverance wrought for the race and the marvelous providences made for its uplift and betterment through all these means, God has been and is constantly appealing as incentives and motives to arouse, stir, persuade and impel the Negro race to loyal devotion and earnest, hearty, faithful, forward movement along the line of Christian progress, righteousness and truth. Though Israel was God's elect, God's peculiar people, and to stress how near they were to Him and how highly favored was the position they once held, Jehovah says: "The Lord's portion in His people; Jacob is the Lot of His inheritance. He found him in a desert land and in the waste howling wilderness; He led him about, He instructed him, He kept him as the apple of His eye." * * * "So the Lord alone did lead him and there was no strange God with him. He made him ride on the high places of the earth that he might eat the increase of the fields; and He made him to suck honey out of the rock, and oil out of the flinty rock."

"But Jeshurun (Israel) waxed fat and kicked * * * then he forsook God which made him, and lightly esteemed the rock of his salvation." Thus Israel in their moral blindness and sinful depravity trampled all the rich mercies of God under their feet, rebelled against His righteous laws, became steeped in iniquity and idolatry and slaves to the love of Mammon and so fell from God's grace, were carried away into captivity, and at last through the destruction of Jerusalem they became rejected and destroyed as an organized nation and church, and scattered among the various Gentile nations of the earth.

And here in this dispersion among the Gentiles without a country, and characterized in prophecy as lost and a valley of dry bones, spiritually dead, Israel, for nearly two thousand years has been allowed to suffer in various ways more severely than any other people in the world. "To whom much is given of him shall much be required." "He that knoweth the law and doeth it not shall be beaten with many stripes; but he that knoweth it not with a few."

Israel as God's elect people stand as a beacon light and blazing warning to all the world, through the direct revelations made to them, the prophecies made through them and fulfilled in them, and the history of God's dealings of mercy and severity with them.

If these people, then, the children of Abraham, of such noble heritage, and for whom God did so much in so many ways, for example, miraculously delivering them from Egyptian bondage, and schooling them at Sinai in the moral, ceremonial and civil laws and thus organizing them as an elect nation, and miraculously feeding and training them in the wilderness forty years and finally planting them as a nation in a land flowing with milk and honey, under heaven made laws and divinely chosen leaders, failed to contend against sin and successfully to resist the flesh, the world and the devil, through failure to watch and pray, to love God supremely, obey him, keep his precepts and commandments and to love their neighbor as themselves--if this people thus failed and were rejected and abolished as an organized church and nation and cast out of Jehovah's sight and buried among heathen nations to suffer for untold centuries in this life and in unmeasured intensity, and millions, perhaps, to be lost and ruined through all eternity; what right, ground or hope has any people less favored by natural heritage, and special divine grace, and less devout and beneficent in service, and less resolute and persistent in battling against the flesh, the world and the devil, for believing, expecting and hoping for

God's special favor, if they fail to profit by all the past; and to seize opportunity, and to yield to the quickening and illuminating light and power of the Holy Spirit, the Living Word and the principles, examples and precepts of Jesus, and thus prove devout, loyal, persistent and faithful soldiers and servants of the cross? What reason, right or ground have they for believing, expecting or hoping that God's dealing with them will be any less terrible, dreadful and severe than it was with Israel? None whatever.

Like the Jew for the last nineteen centuries, the Negro in America, in the world for that matter, is without a country, that is, he has no great, strong civilized nation of his own race to enter into treaty relations with other nations, thus to invest him with increased dignity and to furnish him greater protection of body, property and of life. Hence from every viewpoint the Negro in America, the Negro needs to get right and stay right with God. "For if God be for us who can be against us?" And if we be for

God and remain loyal and true to Him we need never fear; for as in the case of Elisha and his servant at Dothan, they that will be with us as our defenders will be more than they that will be with our enemies. 2 Kings 6:16. Every consideration or reason having to do with the true progress, usefulness and well-being of the race, both in time and eternity, argues with one hundred per cent force that the unquestionable and unfailing duty and the anchoring and eternally saving hope of the individual members and of the race as a whole lies along the pathway of righteousness, of consecrated devotion to God, through saving belief in Jesus as the Son of God and the world's Savior, and through persevering in His service till divinely summoned from labor to reward.

Here lies the path of all that is truly good, eternally safe, elevated and worth while. Here lies the royal path of life where the Negro as a race will find the least opposition from man and the greatest encouragement. Here lies the path along which he can most rapidly and assuredly mend his ways, rise above the dark past, acquire influence, destroy prejudice, win the goodwill of mankind, become desirable citizens, enlist heaven's aid and enjoy heaven's smiles, escape the snares of the devil, overcome carnal weaknesses, honor father and mother and glorify God.

"Ethiopia shall soon stretch out her hands unto God."

Will the younger generation of the Negro race in America follow the path of religious zeal, devotion and growth along which their fathers have trod and rise as much higher and become as much stronger in the great principles of the religion of the triune God as the light they have is brighter and their opportunities are greater?

It is their privilege and duty, but will they? Their own individual needs and the world's needs demand it; but will they? The weight of their increased responsibility demand it; but will they do it? The duty which they owe to their primitive mother land, Africa, demand it; but will they catch the vision, foster the sentiment, rise to the height of the occasion and please heaven and earth by making good? From the character of the reports coming in from a large portion of the leaders of the race in the fields of the home development, public school teaching, Christian evangelism, and Christian teaching, in the higher schools and Sunday Schools, there is demand that much careful and prayerful study be given them.

    These reports clearly indicate that the children in the homes of the race are showing less reverence for parents, less respect for the laws and rules of the home and are less disposed to move promptly and to do faithfully and well what they are told to do than was true of the children of the homes of the race thirty or forty years ago; besides there is less cooperation on the part of parents among themselves for the more effective training of their children.

In the work of public school instruction and government, the same declension is apparent and similar complaint is heard; that the children show less reverence for teachers and for truth and for law and rules and hence are harder to control and to bring under proper discipline than were those of a generation earlier. This in part is a natural result of the failure in the home. When we enter the higher realm of the Christian religion similar reports are heard. The complaints are that the young people of the present generation are becoming less sincere, less inclined to heed good counsel, less devout, that they do not seem to find the joy and comfort in religion that their fathers and mothers found, that they are manifesting less reverence for God, for the Gospel, for religious services and holy things, that in fact, they are becoming decidedly more worldly, more carried away with a craze for dancing, card playing, worldly pleasure and a good time in general in worldly affairs.

These reports, doubtless, should be received with much allowance. But after all is said and done there is in them enough truth to furnish alarm and to serve as timely warning. Indeed the facts of the case, the situation is a stentorian call from earth and heaven to the leaders of the race, to the fathers and mothers, teachers and Gospel ministers and the business leaders of the race, to rally and organize to stem the tide.

The call of earth and heaven is that the fathers and mothers of the different communities must organize among themselves and cooperate for the more efficient training of their children; parents must be urged with all reasonable argument and entreaty to accept and fully live up to the responsibilities of the home. Between teachers and parents there must be hearty and Christian cooperation to secure in the lives of the children the full fruits of the purpose and work of the schools.

Among parents, teachers, Gospel ministers, Sunday School workers, Y. M. C. A. and Y. W. C. A. and other Christian and community workers there should be and must be most hearty, zealous and unflagging cooperation to train up the children in every line of duty in the way they should go.

This can be done ; this should be done; this must be done, if we are to catch the true vision of life's mission, to arouse and foster reasonable race consciousness, pride, affinity and unity; stem the tide, turn the life currents of the race strongly along the royal path of life, realize in a large way the fruition of the prophecy and promise of the text; and thus standing firm upon the Rock Christ Jesus and His infallible word under the guidance of the Holy Spirit, to grow in grace and into that blessed state where God shall have the first place in our life and thought, where we shall love Him supremely and our neighbor as ourself and where we shall be able to love our enemies and pray fervently for those who despitefully use us and persecute us; and thus possess good will toward all men and finally receive the well-done of heaven.

"Ethiopia shall soon stretch out her hands unto God."

Young men and young women of the race, boys and girls, young mothers and fathers, young teachers and leaders of the race, this divine prophecy, promise and appeal is to you. Will you heed it? Will you struggle to realize its promise and enjoy its fruition? Will you watch and pray and cultivate good-will and struggle to lift yourselves and the race out of the slough, the mire of despond into the lifting and saving atmosphere of divine inspiration and growth? Will you cultivate and cherish profound belief in Jesus Christ as the Son of God and the world's Savior? and strive to love God supremely and your neighbor as yourselves? Will you watch, pray and endeavor to teach, inculcate and lead the race of Africa in America and through them, also the race in

Africa to cherish profound faith in God the Father and in His only Son, Jesus our Lord, and in the Holy Ghost as the Comforter? and thus become blessed yourselves and prove a blessing to the race and become a factor in fitting the race to become a blessing to the world of mankind? Will you watch and pray and endeavor to keep a loving and faithful oversight over the homes, public schools and higher schools of the race in which the children and leaders of the race are in training and over the work of the churches, as those possessing race consciousness, race pride and affinity, patriotism and Christian devotion, that under God you may become and prove to be real and important factors in leading the race in a large way to realize the prophecy, promise and appeal of the text and thus to come into the possession of the gracious favor and protection of Jehovah and to move along the royal path of life and thus to accomplish the surest and truest and only enduring progress for time and eternity?

If you will, you can. If you fail as with Israel, awful will be the calamity and suffering in time and unspeakable the woe in eternity. But you will not fail, you dare not fail, you must not fail. Let your motto be that of Joshua: "But as for me and my house we will serve the Lord," and that of Ruth 1:16-17, and that of Paul, Phil. 3:13-14.

GOD HELPING ME I WILL.

A BACCALAUREATE SERMON DELIVERED TO THE GRADUATING CLASS OF LYNCHBURG THEOLOGICAL SEMINARY AND COLLEGE IN THE SPRING OF 1895

Text: In the morning sow thy seed and in the evening withhold not thine hand: for thou knowest not whether shall prosper either this or that or whether they both shall be alike good.--Eccl. 11:6.

SUBJECT: A DILIGENT AND COMPLETE LIFE OF WELL DOING

Young Ladies and Young Men, Class of 1895:

These are beautiful words, beautiful in sound, in symbol, in thought, in the ideas they picture to the mind; but they are most beautiful in the deep, rich truths, which they are designed to vivify, emphasize, inculcate and impress upon the mind, heart and lives of mankind.

The message contained in these words is deeply significant; because of the infinite power of Jehovah, the author, and because of the wisdom, experience, and divine inspiration of the human personality, Solomon, through whom it pleased God to deliver the message, and because of the exalted mission of the people to whom primarily it was delivered, the Jews, God's elect nation, and because of its far-reaching and extensive application, being applicable to the children of men through all the passing centuries.

Let us think of this heavenly message, this morning, as coming directly from Almighty God, through His inspired servant, Solomon, to you and to me, but to you especially as a class just about to enter upon your commencement in life.

The divine message and injunction to you is: "In the morning sow thy seed, and in the evening withhold not thine hand: for thou knowest not whether shall prosper, either this or that, or whether they both shall be alike good."

This message is not only far-reaching and extensive; but it is comprehensive and practical. It applies to boys and girls, men and women, young and old. It applies to every species, form or element of man's complex being, his physical, mental, moral and spiritual being of life.

The author, in order to emphasize and force home the main lesson of the text--that of diligence in well-doing throughout life, makes choice, in mental conception, of the fundamental occupation and the familiar figure and essential servant, the farmer, in action, sowing his seed. The author of the text was a practical man, a careful observer. He used his eyes and his mind, he saw objects and actions and analyzed them and comprehended their meaning. He was a teacher able and experienced. He knew the occupations and the customs of the people. He knew their good qualities and their shortcomings and weaknesses.

He knew that the ideal farmer in seedtime rises and begins sowing his seed in the early morning and that he slacks not his hand in the evening but perseveres with diligence through to the close of the day.

On the other hand, he knew that there are many among farmers and those of all other callings and professions of life, who are good starters, who begin well, who will rise early and start at a rapid pace but as the sun declines towards the west they grow weary, slack their hand, become indifferent, excuse themselves on the ground of what they have done, and thus allow, in the course of days, weeks, months and years, many precious days, weeks, months and even years to be wasted, and the life in so many ways to count very much less than it should, and to fall away below the ideal.

In view of these truths, these human weaknesses and pressing needs of being instructed, aroused and stirred to diligence and perseverance in well-doing, Solomon, from his vantage ground, as king of God's people, and God's servant, takes the ideal farmer, sowing early and sowing late, sowing diligently, faithfully and sowing in hope, sowing his seed that contain life, that shall spring up, bear fruit and bring forth a harvest that shall bless him and his fellowman--he takes this ideal farmer and ideal action and holds them up before the world of mankind to arouse, stimulate and stir boys and girls, men and women to ideal service and action in every phase of life and along all the lines of duty.

Let us notice briefly some duties we owe to ourselves, to our physical, mental, moral and spiritual or religious lives.

Our bodies, individually and physically speaking, are the gift of God and are designed to be the temples of God. It is my duty and your duty to keep the body healthy, "Health is first wealth." A healthy body is the foundation of a healthy and strong development. We owe it not alone to ourselves individually, but to our families, our neighbors, the community, the State, the nation, the world.

The mind, the intellectual life, must be developed and improved. Says one, "There is nothing great in the universe but man and nothing great in man but mind;" and another "The mind is the eyesight of the soul;" another, "The mind is the atmosphere of the soul." Without vision the people perish. Man as important in prompting and stimulating him to do his best needs that enlarged vision and quickening inspiration that come from a well-trained, capacious and a well-stored mind with living, uplifting truths.

But morality or the moral life must be watched and molded with great care and fervent prayer, for the moral life is a round higher in the ladder of human development, human progress. Says one, "Morality is the vestibule of religion." "Morality is essential to good government." "What can laws do without morals?" Says Dr. Horace Mann, "Ten men have failed from defect in morals where one has failed from defect in intellect." Without enlightening the conscience and strengthening the moral sense and moral obligation you can't become good brothers and sisters, good companions, good teachers, good neighbors, good husbands and wives, good fathers and mothers, good citizens.

This brings us to consider the spiritual life, the Christian religious life, which forms the climax of human development, advance and progress. While it is the duty of each both in the morning and evening of the day and of life to watch and guard and preserve and develop the health of the body, to cultivate, enlarge and enrich the mind and to enlighten and strengthen the moral sense, yet it is the spiritual life that brings us into the family of God, links us with all that is brightest and best in eternity.

It is here man's first and highest duties lie. "Thou shalt love the Lord thy God with all thy heart, and with all thy soul and with all thy might." "And thou shalt love thy neighbor as thyself." "Seek ye first the kingdom of God and His righteousness," and we have the promise that all necessary temporal blessings shall be added.

"Bodily exercise profiteth little, but Godliness is profitable unto all things, having promise of the life that now is and of that which is to come." "Remember thy Creator in the days of thy youth."

"Believe on the Lord Jesus Christ and thou shalt be saved." It is by belief in Jesus as the Son of God that one is born unto the Kingdom of God and comes into possession of spiritual life and has communion and fellowship with the triune God and His loyal, faithful servants and is prepared to sow the good seed of which Jesus spoke that fell into good ground and brought forth some an hundred fold.

BACCALAUREATE SERMON DELIVERED TO THE GRADUATING CLASS OF THE CAIRO HIGH SCHOOL, CAIRO, ILL., IN THE SPRING OF 1901

Text: "Therefore whosoever heareth these sayings of mine and doeth them I will liken him unto a wise man which built his house upon a rock."--Matt. 7:24.

SUBJECT: BUILDING FOR TIME AND ETERNITY

The words of the text form a part of the conclusion of the greatest sermon ever preached upon this earth. It was preached upon a memorable occasion. It was preached to a unique company of men under preparation for most exalted service. It was preached by the greatest being who ever tabernacled in human flesh, or whose footsteps ever pressed the surface of this earth, or whose precious blood was ever shed in evidence of ardent love for mankind. It was preached to crystallize for all time some of the richest and most essential truths that have ever contributed to, or entered into the well-being of mankind.

Among the many beautiful, deeply significant and weighty truths therein found are the cardinal and momentous truth and message contained in the words chosen as the basis of principles we hope to emphasize, and lessons we hope to teach and instructions we hope to give, this afternoon to this class of 1901 and to this assembled audience.

The subject is: BUILDING FOR TIME AND ETERNITY.

Life is a great gift and it has a lofty mission. Man is made in the image of God, the crowning work of creation. He was and is endowed with an immortal soul, containing faculties of wonderful possibilities and grave responsibilities.

Hence in view of what man is in his being, in his endowments, in his relations and in his mission, it is clear that life is deeply and profoundly significant and the proper solution of life is a very solemn and weighty problem.

It becomes the bounden duty of man then to make a broad and careful survey of life.

He should survey life from a retrospective view, a prospective view, and from its daily evolutions. He should ponder life frequently, deeply and long. He should ponder it faithfully and prayerfully in his efforts to comprehend its meaning, and measure its claims and value.

He should use the God appointed means. He should pray much for God's favor and the proper frame of mind for profound and lasting impressions. He should read much and study the word of God as quick and powerful, and as a lamp unto his feet and a light upon his path. He should study history, profane, natural and sacred. He should study the natural sciences, the ology's. He should study everything that throws light upon life, its relations, responsibilities, duties, mission and destinies.

God is the author of all being in its different forms, and the laws governing the same. All nature in some way throws light upon God our Maker and Preserver, and upon our relations, duties, and responsibilities to our fellowmen and to Jehovah. "The heavens declare the glory of God and the firmament showeth his handiwork."

But the light from nature was not sufficient, so God gave to mankind a special revelation.

The builder needs a model, the sailor needs a chart, Jesus Christ is our model, the word of God is our chart.

Hence the words: "Therefore, whosoever heareth these sayings of mine and doeth them, I will liken him unto a wise man which built his house upon a Rock," are deeply significant and contain essential instruction. They are a voice from heaven, the voice of God, the author of our being, the Lamb slain from the foundation of the world for our redemption and salvation. He declares we must hear and heed His teaching and build according to His counsel, according to His will, and that they who thus build, build wisely, safely and surely, build for time and eternity.

Now, young people, class of 1901, I am proud to be able to say that by your profession and I am persuaded by your possession you have begun right, wisely and well. In the sublime sermon by the unique Christ are words, "Seek ye first the Kingdom of God and His righteousness and all these things shall be added unto you." In part at least you have been obedient to the divine injunction. You have sought and found the Savior. You have entered into that spiritual state. You have linked your life with the glorious life of eternity.

For these things we are proud of you, we commend you, we congratulate, we praise you, we bid you God speed.

And, too, there is another line along which you are well-begun. Says the inspired sage, natural offspring of David: "A wise man will hear and will increase learning, and a man of undertaking shall attain unto wise counsel." "And in all thy getting get wisdom and understanding."

Now for a number of years you have been engaged in study. You have been obeying the law of your being, the law of the universe, you have been growing. You have been developing, disciplining and training the powers of your mind, and of your soul. All this is in line of building, of preparedness for service.

You are about to enter upon your commencement. The motto, "finished, but just begun," fits your situation well.

The great law of life is service. With many the idea of servant is unpopular. But Jesus says: "Whosoever would be great in his kingdom let him serve; and he that would be chief let him become servant of all."

BACCALAUREATE SERMON DELIVERED TO THE GRADUATING CLASS OF 1909, OF BLUEFIELD, W. VA., JUNE 6, 1909

Text: "Be strong therefore and show thyself a man." 1 Kings 2:2.

"The world's great need is a better man, better women, better manhood, better womanhood."

There are many things that become associated with words in such a way as to give to them special significance. Such is true of the word which I have selected as the basis of what I shall have to say to you as the graduating class of 1909, and to this audience as well.

These words were uttered many centuries ago, more than one thousand years before the Christian era. They were uttered by a man who had inherited well, who was old in years, full of experience, the father of many children, exalted in station, the king of an elect people, devout in service, a man of large achievements both in state and church affairs, and was now at the very gateway of departure out of this life into the paradise of God. From this vantage ground with a flood of light flowing into his soul from a retrospective and prospective view of life and feeling all the weight of exalted station, he uttered these solemn words to his son, "I go the way of all the earth: be thou strong therefore, and show thyself a man."

All through the Holy Scriptures man is used as a generic term including both sexes the male man and the female man, in other words, man and woman.

Hence in the text of our choice we shall think of it and speak of it as sufficiently comprehensive to include both men and women.

Now young men and young women, members of the class of 1909, I would like to have you think of yourselves and regard yourselves as occupying that relation and attitude toward God and men as was true of Solomon at the time these solemn words were addressed to him. And thus regarding yourselves, I would like to have you think of these words addressed from God through the lips of David directly to you: "I go the way of all the earth: be thou strong therefore, and show thyself a man," or show thyselves men virtuous, true, aspiring, patient, persevering, faithful, devout, patriotic, friendly, courageous. Remember that the world's great need is a better man, better woman.

Now, young men and young women, I am glad that your course of conduct puts me in position to say that you have been and are on the right road to help to supply this great need of the world.

You have been engaged for a number of years in developing, disciplining and training the faculties and powers of your body, mind and soul. This is in line with wisdom. It rests on the eternal verities. The Word of God says: "As a man thinketh in his heart, so is he." We know that among the Hebrews, in Bible times, it was customary to think and speak of the heart as we now think and speak of the mind as the seat of thought, reason, understanding. "As a man thinketh in his heart, so is he." Bacon says, "there is nothing great in the universe but man, and nothing great in man but mind," or soul. It is here that we look for the image of God, that eternal principle, or personality that thinks, feels, forms judgments, discriminates between right and wrong, is progressive and in its moral nature or state loves knowledge, aspires after things pure, beautiful, elevating and lofty, approves the good, and condemns and rejects the bad.

In this course of conduct, in this line of development and training, like Abraham of sacred history and father of the faithful, you are being blest yourselves and becoming prepared to be a blessing to others.

As in nature everywhere there are choice blessings that were stored up there centuries ago, and as man has had need of them they have been yielding up their rich fruits to satisfy his every want. And as it is true that over more than half the globe daily there are processes operating in nature, taking inorganic matter and putting it on the plane of organic matter where it is prepared to be and is blessing mankind every day, yes, every hour and every moment. So; in like manner you young men, you young women, every day, month and year, by systematic study and faithful endeavor, have been developing discipling and training faculties, acquiring power and knowledge, and coming into possession of light, wisdom, and other elevating qualities of mind, heart and life that fit you like the dews of heaven to distill blessings upon mankind.

This brings us back to our subject, the world's great need of a better man, better woman, better manhood, better womanhood.

But this better manhood and better womanhood expresses itself in many forms or qualities, in many ways, along many lines in reference to many things.

One of the ways in which it manifests itself and that very significantly is in power, physical, intellectual, moral, spiritual, political, civil, social, financial power.

A TEMPERANCE SERMON DELIVERED BEFORE A S. S. WOMEN'S AND MENS CONVENTION IN MURRAY, KENTUCKY, SEPT 29, 1905

Text: Prov. 20:1; Jer. 35:6; Psalms 37:37.

In this sermon on temperance, while I shall speak somewhat of temperance in all things and shall strive to emphasize and urge the importance of the same, yet the gist, core, and burden of what I shall have to say shall be concerning temperance or total abstinence from the use of alcoholic or intoxicating liquors as a beverage.

Intemperance in the use and abuse of alcoholic or intoxicating liquors as a beverage has become so prevalent, so widespread and such a gigantic and monstrous evil, in the home, the State, the nation, the church and in the world, that it has almost exclusively appropriated the idea contained in the word temperance.

So that whenever we speak of a temperance sermon, lecture or temperance campaign, we at once understand it to be a sermon lecture or campaign against the use and abuse of alcoholic or intoxicating liquors as a beverage, or against the evil of intoxicating liquors in every form.

The Scripture texts selected as a basis of what I shall have to say first gives us heaven's declaration of the pernicious character of intoxicating liquors, the insanity of those who indulge in the use of them as beverages, that is as mere pleasurable drinks, and gives us heaven's warning against the use of intoxicating liquors as drinks. Secondly, there is furnished us the beautiful example of the Rechabites in their loyal, faithful, steadfast obedience to the instruction of their father Jonadab.

The sacred record tells us: "The Word came unto Jeremiah from the Lord, saying, Go unto the house of the Rechabites, and speak unto them, and bring them unto the house of the Lord, into one of the chambers and give them wine to drink. This instruction was carried out. There was set before the whole company of the Rechabites, pots full of wine and cups, and they were invited to drink.

"But they said, We will drink no wine," "for Jonadab the son of Rechab our father commanded us, saying, Ye shall drink no wine, neither ye, nor your sons forever." * * * "Thus have we obeyed the voice of Jonadab the son of Rechab our father in all that he hath charged us, to drink no wine all our days, we, our wives, our sons, nor our daughters." This beautiful example of the Rechabites by Jehovah through his servant Jeremiah is spread before the Jews or Judah to shame them and condemn their rank disobedience to God's repeated and most solemn and urgent commands. In like manner it is intended as wholesome instruction to mankind through all the centuries.

The words of Psalms 37:37, "Mark the perfect man and behold the upright; for the end of that man is peace!" are used so often in funeral sermons and services of the dead that it may seem strange to use them as a text for a temperance sermon.

But we want you to think at this hour and in these days much of crucifixion, death and burial.

The taste and desire for intoxicating liquors and the habit of of drinking them, by every sensible person ought to be fought to the death. True temperance means the death and burial of many evil passions, appetites, desires and bad habits.

And in this sermon on this occasion I shall urge directly and indirectly, all members of the Christian families, especially, and others as well, to enter strenuously upon the work of crucifying passions, desires, and appetites for intoxicating liquors, and to foster the sentiments and taste and to practice the habits of temperance.

Briefly, some strong reasons why all mothers and fathers, sisters and brothers, why all children, teachers, officers, Sunday School teachers and especially ministers of the Gospel should totally abstain from the use of intoxicating liquor as a drink.

Science condemns the use of alcoholic or intoxicating liquors as a drink. The books on "Healthy Body" in the public schools all over the land condemn it as a poison to the tissues. By the most careful and thorough analysis and experiments it has been demonstrated beyond doubt that alcohol or intoxicating liquors in both small and large quantities tend to injure, impair and weaken the life-giving cells, to impair and weaken the actions of the heart, the liver, the kidneys, the muscles, the stomach, the brain, the nerves, the mind, the whole man.

Science shows also that intoxicating liquors have the power of creating an uncontrollable appetite for themselves; hence another reason why so dangerous. Science shows also that intoxicating liquors are a prolific source of insanity, poverty, and crime, of widows, orphans and wretchedness.

Economic statistics condemn the use of intoxicating liquors as a beverage, as a prolific waste of money, hundreds of millions yearly.

The business world condemns their use. Men are rendered unsafe and untrustworthy.

The Christian church condemns their use. Men are made very immoral.

The Holy Scripture all through condemns their use, leads even and often to the loss of souls. 1 Cor. 6:10.

SERMON DELIVERED TO THE WOMAN'S BAPTIST STATE CONVENTION IN SESSION AT HINTON, WEST VIRGINIA, AUGUST, 1917

Text: Let her alone; why trouble ye her? She hath done what she could.--Mark 14:6, 8.

She hath done what she could--

This is a weighty declaration. It was made on a memorable occasion by our Lord Jesus, the greatest human personality in history. It was addressed to men under training for the highest mission ever committed to mankind by the author of all being.

The words of the text and subject contain for the men, for the disciples of Christ a rebuke intended to reprove and sober them in thought and judgment. For the conduct of the disciples on this occasion shows, despite the fact they had been in a

Christian school under the training of Christ Himself the Master Teacher for about three years, that yet they were very imperfect, narrow, selfish, bigoted and blind.

An act intrinsically beautiful and far-reaching in significance to them seemed worthy only of harsh and condemning criticism.

How often the same is true today. Before we know anything about the facts, the nature of the case, or motives prompting the act or the end aimed at we plunge in with adverse criticism, seeking to tear down and destroy rather than to build up and save.

But honest and sober thought usually reveal a beam in our own eye as the actuating cause. Every such occasion invites to self-examination and prayer.

"Let her alone; why trouble ye her * * * She hath done what she could."

These words mark the beginning of that leveling among the children of men that Christianity was and is designed to accomplish as foretold in prophecy: "The voice of him that crieth in the wilderness, Prepare ye the way of the Lord, make straight in the desert a highway for our God. "Every valley shall be exalted and every mountain and hill shall be made low: and the crooked shall be made straight and the rough paces plain." Isa. 40:3-4.

This brings us to speak of a

LIFE OF COMPLETE SERVICE TO CHRIST.

We wish to consider:

- 1. What such service is.
- 2. Why it should be given.
- 3. How it should be given.
- 4. The results.

1. What such service is; what it consists in.

In giving to Christ and His service our purest and deepest affection--love.

Where there is love, there is interest, keen, inspiring, lasting. Affliction becomes light and duties sweet.

The soul that feeds on love grows upon what it feeds, and such a soul is on the road to a frame of mind and state of being, where it can largely realize and appreciate the lofty sentiments of the ancient Hebrew rabbis expressed in the words:

"Joy is duty, so with golden lore,
The Hebrew rabbis taught in days of yore.
And happy human hearts heard in their speech
Almost the highest wisdom man can reach."

Yet still rising far above is the voice of one whose name is love, teaching those whom His words employ. Life is divine when duty is a joy. Joy then is the fruit of love, that greatest thing in the world which scatters seeds of kindness and sends forth rays of sunshine along life's pathway.

2. Why a life of complete and full service to Christ should be given.

(a) Because God commands it.

"Hear, O Israel! the Lord our God is one Lord: And thou shalt love the Lord thy God with all thy heart, and with all thy soul and with all thy might." "And thou shalt love thy neighbor as thyself." "Whatsoever thy hand findeth to do do with thy might." "Life is the time to serve the Lord; the time to insure the great reward."

"She hath done what she could." "This measures up to the exact requirement." "She built for herself and for the world a monument and obtained the approval and the praise of Jesus." "She built better than she knew." "Jesus said: 'Verily I say unto you whosesoever this Gospel shall be preached throughout the whole world, this also, that this woman hathe done shall be spoken of for a memorial of her.'"

3. How a life of complete and full service to Christ is to be given.

Christ is the Christian's model and the Bible is the chart of life.

Hence obedience lies at the foundation. "Search the Scriptures, for in them ye think ye have eternal life, and they are they that testify of me." "Watch and pray." "Pray without ceasing." "Men ought always to pray and not to faint."

"Prayer is the Christian's vital breath,
　The Christian's native air;
　His watchword at the gate of death,
　He enters heaven with prayer."

　　The Christian must have power with God and man. Bloody Mary is reported to have said: "I fear the prayers of John Knox more than all the armies of Europe." "There seemed good reason for this fear." "Bloody Mary's removal from the throne of England seemed a direct answer to prayer."

　　4. The results.

　　She hath done what she could. This foreshadowed the work of women under the Christian dispensation. The required study of the evil effects of alcoholic liquors and narcotics on the human system, in the public schools of the United States and the 18th Amendment are both largely due to woman's work. Her opportunity for good and influence are constantly growing.

A SERMON DELIVERED TO A SUNDAY SCHOOL WOMAN'S AND MEN'S CONVENTION AT NEW MADRID, MISSOURI, AND AT THE W. VA. WOMAN'S BAPTIST STATE CONVENTION, CHARLESTON, W. VA., (1) 1906; 2 (1912)

Text: Ruth 1:16-17.

The story of Ruth is said to be one of the most pathetic, sweet and beautiful to be found anywhere in the Bible, or in any other form of literature.

"Intreat me not to leave thee, nor to return from following after thee: for whither thou goest I will go, and where thou lodgest I will lodge; thy people shall be my people, and thy God my God. Where thou diest will I die, and there will I be buried. The Lord do so to me and more also if aught but death part thee and me."

These are great words. They are great because of the beautiful sentiments and scene which they bring before the mind. They are great because of the circumstances under which they were uttered.

In the last three chapters of Judges, 18-21, is found the story of the Levite, a horrible story, showing the very worst phase or condition of life in the time of the Judges.

This period is one of the blackest to be found anywhere in the history of God's people and of the world.

"But night brings out the stars," and, "Behind a frowning providence God hides a smiling face."

So in this period of moral darkness and gloom in the history of God's people the book of Ruth reveals characters that shine forth as the noonday sun, and from whose lives and utterances truths have become crystallized that have been quickening life, kindling interest and zeal, stirring hearts and inspiring souls with increased vision, light, admiration, love, hope and desire to rise and accomplish good through the centuries.

We wish to consider:

1. That from which Ruth was climbing and lifting as she climbed.

Ruth at the time she uttered these charming and soul-stirring words, was coming out from and separating herself from her natural, heathen and sinful kinsmen, and was renouncing her heathen Gods and heathen religion. In this noble and blessed action she was tried, she was put to the test. For in the journey of Naomi from Moab back to Bethlehem-Judah after her daughters-in-law, Orpah and Ruth, according to the customs of the times, had accompanied her a part of the way, she entreated them, in most pathetic and persuasive terms, to return to their people.

She said to her two daughters-in-law, go, return each to her mother's house: the Lord deal kindly with you as ye have dealt with the dead and with me. The Lord grant you that ye may find rest, each of you in the house of her husband. Then she kissed them and they lifted up their voices and wept.

Orpah, under the power of the entreaty and the strength of home, country, and kindred attachments, returned, but Ruth reached a decision that is charmingly beautiful and of eternal worth, and she expressed and clothed this decision in language so rich, elegant, lofty, firm and of such intrinsic worth that tens of thousands through the centuries have been led by its beauty, charm, power and uplift to the better life of the true religion and to walk and work in the light and service of God the Father and Jesus Christ His only Son.

2. The way along which and by which she was climbing and lifting as she climbed.

Jesus said, I am the way, I am the light of the world.

Ruth was climbing along that way that leads from darkness to light, from bondage to liberty, from degradation to salvation.

Ruth had not only come out from and separated herself from her own heathen and sinful kind men and renounced her heathen gods and heathen religion, but she had espoused the true God and the true religion and was associating herself with God's people. She was moving on the upward way.

Moses, as leader of Israel, was leading them from the bondage and moral religious darkness of Egypt through the trials of the wilderness towards the land of milk and honey and towards the light and saving power and influence of the true God. So Ruth in following Naomi was being led away from darkness to light, from false gods to the true God, from immorality to righteousness.

3. The goal of Ruth's climbing and lifting as she climbed was Canaan, God's country, and Judah, God's people and true religious fellowship and service. God's

service as a type of heaven and its God, people, and service.

Faith in God, His word and service was the rock upon which she built; faith is the soil in which has grown the most efficacious and blessed fruit of the ages.

Any weakling can doubt. But the men and women who have been instrumental in lifting the world heavenward have been men and women of strong faith, as Abraham, Moses, Joshua, Job, David. And women like Ruth, who could say, "Entreat me not to leave thee." And like Hannah, mother of Samuel. And like Esther and Mary Magdalene.

A SERMON DELIVERED AT THE WEST VIRGINIA BAPTIST STATE CONVENTION AT BECKLEY, W. VA., IN AUGUST, 1912

Study or give diligence to render thyself approved unto God, a workman that needeth not to be ashamed, handling aright, or rightly dividing, the word of truth. 2 Tim. 2:15.

Study, give diligence to become a Gospel minister and Christian workman approved unto God.

These words were addressed by the great apostle Paul to Timothy, his own spiritual son in the Gospel.

At the time when he uttered or wrote these words he was old in years, rich in experience, devout and consecrated in life and character, energetic in Christian service, farseeing in wisdom, heroic in courage, anchored in the hope of the Gospel and the eternity of the blessed life beyond.

I wish this morning to consider:

1. What we should study.

All study of whatever kind should be with the view and purpose of making the Gospel minister's preaching, life and work, most effective, and thus securing God's approval.

Study, give diligence.

Study books, arts, sciences.

Study self (psychology, physiology, etc.).

Study others (history, sociology, etc.).

Study things (physics, chemistry, botany, zoology).

Study God (theology, religion, spirituality).

Above all, study the plain, simple Scriptures, the inspired Word of God.

I But we must never forget that: "The heavens declare the glory of God; and the firmament showeth His handiwork. Day unto day uttereth speech, and night unto night showeth knowledge. There is no speech nor language where their voice is not heard."

Hence God speaks to the children of men through the whole realm of nature, of the created universe as well as through His special divine revelation.

Permit me to say here that I believe in an educated and trained ministry, and in an educated and intelligent pew or laity, and that the surest and best way to have an educated and intelligent pew or laity is to have an educated and well trained ministry.

This is no reflection on that large class of uneducated and untrained ministers that have done such a large and creditable work in the Master's vineyard, only as they have through indifference and willfulness neglected education and training and in some cases have gone so far as to deny its importance.

    2. Why we should study, why we should give diligence.

- 1. Because God commands it.
- 2. Because the individual minister needs it.
- 3. Because the Christian church needs it.
- 4. Because the world needs it.

God, speaking to His servant Ezekiel, said, Thou son of man, hear what I say unto thee; be not thou rebellious like that rebellious house: open thy mouth and eat that I give thee, And when I looked, said Ezekiel, behold an hand was sent unto me, and lo a roll of a book was therein; And He spread it before me; and in it was written within and without, and there was written therein lamentations and mournings and woe. Moreover he said unto me, son of man eat that thou findest, eat this roll, and go speak unto the house of Israel. So I opened my mouth and He caused me to eat that roll. And he said unto me, Son of man, cause thy belly to eat, and fill thy bowels with this roll that I give thee. Then did I eat it, and it was in my mouth as honey for sweetness. And He said unto me son of man go, get thee unto the house of Israel and speak with my words unto them.

This language makes it very plain that the minister of the Gospel is to strive to master the message he is to preach, that he is to analyze, digest and to become saturated and filled with the Word of God itself and then present it as a warm message from God to man, from God to the people.

Now just as God commanded Ezekiel to eat the roll, the word, the message, to digest it and to become saturated and filled with it and then speak to the people, so He commands you and me. Ezekiel obeyed, so must you, so must I. Obedience is the gateway to God's favor, to God's approval.

Study, give diligence. The minister of the Gospel himself needs it, in order to do his best and be his best. All through the Old Testament's sacrifices and offerings God demanded the best.

Behold to obey is better than sacrifice and to hearken than the fat of rams.

3. That in view of which or the purposes for which we should study, give diligence.

To become master workmen, to gain larger vision of truth. "Where there is no vision the people perish." Study, give diligence, to have the living Word kindle a flame of zeal and sacred love in our soul, to cause our light to shine bright, to become more faithful and fervent in prayer and thus to come into possession of more power with God and man, that by all means we might become instrumental in God's hands of saving some.

SCHOOL FOR WOMEN AND GIRLS, LINCOLN HEIGHTS, D. C., IN THE SUMMER OF 1918

Text: If ye continue in my word then are ye my disciples indeed; and ye shall know the truth and the truth shall make you free. John 8:31-32.

FREEDOM THROUGH THE TRUTH

I wish to direct your attention this afternoon to the subject: "Freedom through the truth."

And I wish to consider the divine message contained in the text under two main heads.

- I. The Condition.
- If ye continue in my word.
- II. The Promises.
- 1. Then are ye my disciples indeed.
- 2. And ye shall know the truth.
- 3. And the truth shall make you free.

Looking backward as we review the past, we find two great classes of humanity. The one class is represented by such characters as Enoch, Noah, Abraham, Joseph, Moses, Joshua, Gideon, Ruth, Esther, Hannah, Samuel, the prophets, apostles, martyrs and pilgrims. This class have not been wedded to this world, but they have had conceptions of a belief in something better, grander, nobler. Hence, they have been progressive and struggled to realize high ideals, to bless mankind, and to lift the world upward.

The other class is represented by such as Cain, Ishmael, Esau, Pharaoh, the Sodomites, Philistines, Caananites, and the proud, haughty and disobedient and rebellious of all ages.

This class has been short-sighted, wedded to this world and has been able to see little good in anything that does not minister to carnal appetite and selfishness.

When Jesus uttered the words of the text He was in the temple at Jerusalem. It was in the course of passion week and two great throngs were about Him, and the two classes of whom we have spoken were there. Jesus taught them many things, uttering some of His richest, deepest and most salient truths, telling them whence He was, why He had come into the world, that He is the light of the world, and as He spoke many believed on him. "Then said Jesus to those Jews which believed on Him: If you continue in my word, then are ye my disciples indeed, and ye shall know the truth and the truth shall make you free."

1. Let us consider the condition (if you continue in my word).

Life is progressive. This is true of all life. It is especially true of the Christian life. Grow in grace and in the knowledge of the Lord Jesus. The Christian life is spiritual, the highest type of life. The best and greatest things grow slowly. Only mushrooms grow up in a night, but the oak, the cedars of Lebanon that stand highest on the mountain, have been growing for centuries.

If ye continue in my word. This Christian life is a race and must be run with patience, endurance, long-suffering. The race is not to the swift, nor the battle to the strong, but to those that endure to the end. There are many good starters in worthy enterprises but they fail in the end, like Amaziah and Uzziah. If ye continue in my word then are ye my disciples indeed.

II. The Promises:

1. Then are ye my disciples indeed.

Jesus Christ is the world's great teacher. He is unique as teacher, and His school was and is an unique Christian school. Those who enter this school are His disciples. Those who continue are His disciples indeed. The way of the disciples of Christ is spoken of as a highway, as a narrow way, as a way of self-denial and sacrifice, as a way of trimming off fruitless branches, and purging those that bear fruit, as a way in which the old life of lying, stealing, profanity, and corruption is put off, and of putting on the new life of Christian veracity, honesty, holiness and purity. These lessons every human soul or immortal soul needs to learn and must learn if he continues in the school of Jesus.

2. And ye shall know the truth.

Ye shall know that I am the promised seed of the woman that should bruise the serpent's head, that I am the promised seed of Abraham by which all the families of the earth should be blessed, that I am that prophet of whom Moses spoke and whom Isaiah wrote saying: "He was wounded for our transgressions, He was bruised for our iniquities, the chastisement of our peace was upon him, and with His stripes we are healed," that I am what I claim to be, the Jewish Messiah, the long expected one, the only begotten Son of God and the world's

Savior. These are among the golden truths of the world.

3. And the truth shall make you free.

Free from the guilt or penalty of sin, for belief in Jesus delivers from the guilt or penalty of sin, and our suffering falls on Jesus. He suffered in our stead, the just for the unjust. He paid it all, all the debt we owe; freedom from the power, love, corruption of sin. O, what a glorious freedom; freedom from the fear of death, freedom from the wrath of God, freedom from the fear of the great enemy of all good.

Bless the Lord, O my soul, and all that is within me bless His holy name!

EXTRACTS FROM AN ADDRESS AT THE CELEBRATION OF FIFTY YEARS OF FREEDOM OF THE NEGRO RACE IN AMERICA, HILL TOP, FAYETTE COUNTY, W. VA., APRIL 9, 1913

Mr. President, Ladies and Gentlemen:

Fifty years ago the 22nd of September, the famous Emancipation Proclamation by Abraham Lincoln was issued. Fifty years ago last January 1st, that Proclamation went into legal effect. On the 9th of April fifty years ago today Gen. Robt. E. Lee, who had been the soul of the rebellion with the remnant of his army, on the field of Appomattox, surrendered to Gen. U. S. Grant.

This removed all organized resistance to the Union and marks this day in the minds of many as the day of greatest memorial significance in the deliverance of the Negro from American slavery.

This depends, however, much on conception, faith in God and the triumph of truth, and the strength of patriotic sentiment.

All the days: September 22nd, January 1st, and April 9th, are of blessed memory and deserve to have their memories cherished.

The real benefit, however, that is to be derived by us as a race, and by others through us from the celebration of one or all of these days is the development in our souls of a deeper sense of the worth and a higher appreciation of the very great privilege and blessing of liberty.

It is by contrast that we gain clearest views and receive deepest and most lasting impressions. The present sinks its roots deep in the past, and in order to know and properly value the present we must study and know much of the past. Says a great scholar: "There is no greater calamity that can befall any people than to be forgetful or ignorant of their past."

God established among the Israelites the Feast of Tabernacles to keep them mindful of their camping, marches, and trials in the wilderness. Says Patrick Henry, "I know of no way of judging the future but by the past," and looking at the blessings of liberty above slavery said, "Give me liberty or give me death." We would note and emphasize first of all the very significant truth: that from January, 1863, to the close of the war, 1865, about two hundred thousand Negro troops were enlisted in the U. S. army and navy, and that in the course of these years they fought heroically on many battlefields and in many naval contests. This circumstance furnished to the Negro a happy vantage ground. It put him in the dignified position of patriotic and loyal subject, of putting his life on the altar of his country, to help save the Union, to secure his own liberty, and that of others, and to make this country indeed and in truth "The land of the free and the home of the brave."

This patriotic and heroic service to his country, lifted the Negro much in the minds of many, softened prejudice, made many friends and paved the way for the framing and adoption of the 13th, 14th and 15th Amendments to the U. S. Constitution and the passage of the Civil Rights Bill. But with the fall of the Confederacy, April 9th, 1865, at Appomattox, nearly 4,000,000 persons of African descent in this country were legally and more or less physically free, that is, they could not be bought and sold. They belonged to themselves and had the right to contract and to receive the compensation for their services.

But under the bond and handicap of illiteracy, superstition, poverty, prejudice, jealousy, lack of homes, of confidence, of experience in business and self-direction, amid a hostile and aggressive people, were left this nearly 4,000,000 freedmen. The question naturally arose, "What will we do with the Negro?" "What must the Negro be taught to do for himself?"

Some fifty or more Freedmen's Aid Societies and active organizations by the government and the various Christian denominations were formed, and centers of distress were established at Port Royal, Fortress Monroe, Washington, New Orleans, Vicksburg, and Corinth, Miss., and Columbus, Ky., and Cairo, Ill., and elsewhere.

These centers of distress were at first under control of the treasury department. Later they were turned over to the army officials. Here the work was advanced somewhat along systematic lines by enlisting able bodied men and giving work to others. Confiscated and abandoned estates South and West were leased to superintendents or organizations and given over to the freedmen for cultivation.

The government and benevolent societies furnished the means and thus the great body of freedmen returned slowly to work. The system of control thus started rapidly grew here and there into strange little governments like that of Gen. Banks in Louisiana, with its 90,000 black subjects, is 50,000 guided laborers and its annual budget of $100,000 or more. Other systems of control like this might be mentioned that covered a wider range of territory and whose workings are given more in detail.

It was from these systems that Gen. Armstrong and Gen. Howard got their conception and caught the inspiration that led to the establishment of Hampton Institute and Howard University.

The powers of the Freedmen's Bureau were enlarged in 1865, and given its final form in 1866. It continued till 1869. This bureau brought all these little systems heretofore mentioned under one central control. Gen. O. O. Howard of Maine appointed May 12, 1865, was commissioner of this new bureau and began promptly the work of his office. The bureau invited continued cooperation with benevolent societies. Nine commissioners were appointed and the object of all was: (1) to introduce practical systems of compensated labor; (2) to establish schools; (3) gradually to close relief establishments and to make the destitute self-supporting; (4) to act as courts of law where there were no courts; (5) to establish the institution of marriage among ex-slaves; (6) to keep records; (7) to see that freedmen were free to choose their employers and to help to make contracts for them; (8) to sell confiscated public land for school property.

The task was gigantic.

After a year's work pushed most vigorously as it was the task seemed more difficult to grasp and solve than at the beginning. There were three things done in the first years well worth doing: (1) it relieved a vast amount of physical suffering; (2) it transported 7,000 fugitives from congested centers back to the farm; (3) best of all, it inaugurated the crusade of the New

England school ma'am and the outpouring of Northern benevolence.

The work of the New England school ma'am and Northern benevolence has been denominated "The Ninth Crusade." It is a most interesting story. They did their work. In that first year, it is estimated they taught 1,000,000 souls. Space forbids our going further with this interesting story of reconstruction, readjustment and development.

The opposition to the Negro's development by Southern ex-slave holders and others had to be overcome. But despite it all the progress of the Negro in fifty years has no parallel in history. He has increased in numbers to 10,000,000, reduced illiteracy from ninety percent to thirty-eight per cent, growth in wealth, 337,000 farms owned in their own right, 409,717 farmed under the control as tenants, the number of acres thus controlled and owned, 38,233,933, taxable property from $600,000,000 to

$800,000,000; 23462 church buildings, 23,770 church organizations.

AN ADDRESS DELIVERED ON THE 105TH ANNIVERSARY OF THE BIRTHDAY OF ABRAHAM LINCOLN IN MEMORY AND HONOR OF HIS GREAT LIFE AND SERVICES, AT McDONALD, W. VA., 1914

Ladies and Gentlemen, Members of Sunday School Unions and Forward Movement Clubs, Citizens of Fayette County and Elsewhere: We have met here on this night of the 105th anniversary of the birthday of Abraham Lincoln to celebrate the day, the birth, and the life of that great man. It is highly fitting that we should do so. Longfellow says:

"The lives of great men all remind us
 We may make our lives sublime,
 And departing leave behind us
 Footprints on the sands of time."

Life itself is so marvelous and endowed with such great possibilities that, if lived as is possible to each and every individual human being to whom is vouchsafed an average life, that life may be truly said to be sublime.

Another great man has said: "The world's greatest need is a better man." This statement is attested by the fact that "In the beginning God created man in His own image," upright, and when by transgression he fell God gave to the world in the person of His Son a perfect man for its redemption, example and eternal salvation. The goal is set before us, the need is ever present with us. Duty is pressing and vocal in its call to man to aim high, rise and shine. But in rising, in climbing the ladder of progress, development and hope, man must have something upon which to fix his vision and to which to cling for inspiration, quickening interest, and to give light, brace and strength.

In observing the lives of others we can better see our own lives. In tracing the paths that others have trod we can better see and learn our own way through the world.

In viewing and reviewing the deeds and achievements of others, especially of the great, we are permitted in thought and vision to pass through the great and stirring scenes of the past, to sit and stand, and to walk and talk with the great and worthy, and thus to receive impressions that are lasting, to have our minds illumined, stirred afresh, our sluggish natures aroused, our blood warmed and our wills moved to the sticking point of greater resolves, endeavors and achievements.

Prof. Kelley Miller, in his "Race Adjustment" under the head of "Eminent Negroes," says: "The glory of any people is perpetuated and carried forward by the illustrious names which spring from among them."

The great character whose birth, life and deeds we have met to celebrate, tonight, according to historic genealogy, was not of us as a race. But his lowly birth and humble surroundings; his early privations and small opportunities, his rugged battle against hardships and his glorious triumph over them; his hatred of slavery and all oppression, his strong and telling letters and speeches against the accursed institution; his patriotism, courage, humor and genius in steering the ship of state through the fearful ordeal of a most perplexing and cruel Civil War, and the wisdom displayed in the emancipation of four million slaves and the unspeakable blessing accruing therefrom to the freedmen, to the race at large, and to the wide, wide world--these things, these facts, ideas, acts, principles, deeds and achievements make the life of Abraham Lincoln cosmopolitan in character, akin to all mankind in relation, and a blessed heritage to the whole human race.

The life of Abraham Lincoln then belongs to all races; it belongs to the world.

He was born in a log cabin near Hodgensville, now Hardin County, Kentucky, Feb. 12, 1809.

Lowly birth is no bar to greatness, but it does involve struggle, dogged persistence, unflagging courage and anchoring hope.

But as man struggles, battles and triumphs, strength and experience go into the nerves, muscles, soul and life.

His father moved with his family into the wilderness near Gentryville, Ind. Lincoln has learned to swing the axe at eight years of age. This proves an early instrument of his progress. There is no royal road to greatness. "There is but one method and that is hard labor."

His mother dies, age 35, in 1818, when Lincoln was but nine years old. This, though a sad misfortune, yet for Lincoln there was involved in it another element of independence.

His father married again in 1819. Says one: "The boy Lincoln from eight years of age with the axe as instrument and prophecy of his advance till of age, literally chopped and hewed his way forward and upward." "He learned to read by the light of burning pine knots at night from two books, the spelling book and Bible. Then he borrowed Pilgrim's Progress and Aesop's Fables and would sit up half the night and read them by the blaze of the logs his own axe had split."

The life of this great man is cosmopolitan and rich in every way. Young men, young women, study this life. Don't fail, don't fail.

AN ADDRESS: "THE IMPORTANCE OF THE SUNDAY SCHOOL AND ITS WORK," DELIVERED BEFORE THE W. VA. SUNDAY SCHOOL CONVENTION AT RONCEVERTE, W. VA., MAY 1-3, 1910

The Sunday School is a great institution. Its work is strategic, it is with the children and the young people especially. Too much stress cannot be put upon the importance of this work. To deal with the mind when it is in its formative and plastic state, when impression may be made comparatively easy, deep and lasting, when the mind is vigorous and growing and the habits are forming and the character is in the process of being moulded and taking on fixed form, when lofty ideals and right principles can be most easily and successfully implanted, cultivated and developed, and right sentiments awakened and strengthened, a privilege and opportunity of greatest moment.

The subjects in the lessons and work of the Sunday School which the minds of the children and young people are led to consider, to think about, talk about and feed upon are among the most noble, lofty, grand and sublime that it is possible to conceive of or deal with.

Jesus Christ is the great center around whom all things else are made to revolve. "He is the first and the last." "He is the rose of Sharon and the lily of the valley." He is the bright morning star. He is the lamb slain from the foundation of the world; that taketh away the sins of the world. He is the Redeemer and Savior. He is the one who has been our help in the ages past and is our hope for the years to come. Around Him are encircled the great souls: Abraham, Isaac, Jacob, Joseph, Moses, Aaron, Joshua, Caleb, Samuel, David, Isaiah, Jeremiah, Daniel, Mary, the mother of Jesus, Mary Magdalene, Mary and Martha, sisters of Lazarus, John the Baptist, the twelve disciples, Paul and his spiritual son, Timothy.

What lessons of redeeming love, of saving faith, patience, meekness, long suffering, of loyalty, virtue, self-sacrifice, self-denial, of heroic leadership and lofty, beautiful and sublime teaching, on the one hand, the offspring of infinite love. On the other, what horrible calamities, wretchedness, murder, slaughter and every form of treachery, disobedience, corruption, crime and wickedness, the offspring of sin, come before the mind to awaken and stimulate the best that is in the soul and kindle a love and longing for the good and beautiful and to awaken, foster and grow sentiments that shall dread, abhor and shun the bad, ugly and ruinous!

What stalwart giants of righteousness! What leaders of men! What champions of truth and of the highest interests and well-being of mankind are portrayed in the Sunday School lessons to the minds of the children and young people! Can anyone contemplate such lives, muse upon such deeds, trace the careers of such lofty characters without being instructed, impressed and inspired with sentiments of emulation, of love for the true and the beautiful, and with desire to be better, truer and nobler.

Now in order that we may better see, more keenly feel and appreciate these great privileges, advantages and opportunities and duties as well, we hold conventions, where leaders in this great work may be brought together, exchange ideas, re-hear reasons, review the needs of mankind, the claims and duties devolving upon each to work for others, and to be impressed anew with the value there is in certain lines of work as a means of uplifting and saving the human race.

The history of the progress of the human race has shown to have human hearts, minds and souls stirred more deeply and lasting interest in any work of great importance, of great significance to become strong, warm and fixed that the leaders must be brought together reasonably often in associations and convention with these definite ends in view. Hence the importance and wisdom of these annual Sunday School conventions where the workers from East, West, North and South, from the schools of the churches of different associations and corresponding delegates from other religious bodies meet together to tell of their experiences and observations, and to give expression to their best judgment and thought and offer their best suggestions concerning the advancement and improvement of the work.

It is often found that in many Sunday Schools much time is wasted in discussing questions having no connection with the lesson, or on questions of minor importance.

Again, in many Sunday Schools there is signal failure in bringing the lesson right home to the class and applying its practically.

In the Scriptures we are taught to "train up a child in the way he should go, and when he is old he will not depart from it." To lead the child and the young to accept Christ is the first and highest duty of the teacher.

A SKETCH OF HARPER'S FERRY

"Harper's Ferry, in Jefferson County, is situated at the extreme point of the Eastern Panhandle of West Virginia, at the base of the Blue Ridge Mountains, where the State line converges with the lines of Virginia and Maryland, at the famous gap marking the entrance to the rich and beautiful Valley of Virginia at the confluence of the Potomac and Shenandoah rivers."

The town is about fifty-five miles from Washington, eighty-one from Baltimore, and ninety-six from Cumberland, Md., and is noted for the unrivaled beauty of its natural scenery and for its historical significance. "The place was first mentioned in 1719 in the Chronicles of Virginia as Shenandoah Falls." "It was also known among the squatters of the hills as 'The Hole.' Peter Stevens, a Pennsylvanian, is mentioned as the first squatter. Robt. Harper, for whom the town was named was born in Oxford, England, in 1703, and came to Harper's Ferry in 1747.

Harper purchased the squatters' claims, besides a large tract of land from the Lord Fairfax grant for 60 guineas in gold. In 1763 the town was incorporated as Harper's Ferry by the General Assembly of Virginia. Robt. Harper died in 1782, and is buried in the Harper cemetery on Camp Hill."

"In 1796 Gen. Washington purchased from the Harper family 125 acres of land to be used for an armory site. Washington himself made the survey and draft, recognizing the value of the splendid water power there--said by some to be the finest in the United States."

Later the government purchased 300 acres consisting of Bolivar Heights and Woodland on Loudon Heights. "In 1839 the B.& O. R. R. agreed to pay for the privilege of crossing the Wager Bridge at the Ferry." "Later the railroad company bought the ferry." "The B.& O. bridge at the junction of the rivers being the key which unlocked the treasures of the valley of Virginia was destroyed nine times during the Civil War, and the town itself changed from Union to Confederate hands eight times."

In the same year, 1796, or very soon thereafter the government commenced the erection of shops and other buildings along both rivers as a part of arsenal and armory works, and a Mr. Perkins, an English Moravian, was appointed to superintend the works. From this time till the breaking out of the Civil War the government works here furnished an important source of livelihood for the citizens of the town.

SOME NATURAL SCENERY AND HISTORIC FACTS OR EVENTS OF SPECIAL INTEREST

"On one side of the quaint little town Maryland Heights rise to an altitude of 2,000 feet above sea level; on the Virginia side are the less lofty but equally picturesque and historic Loudon Heights." Much interesting history is connected with these heights. Going back somewhat northwest from the extreme east point of Harper's Ferry along the Bluff overlooking the Potomac, one comes first to Magazine Hill, so named because here at one time the government had a large powder magazine. "On the very edge of the bluff at its highest point commanding one of the finest views in the country, stands the beautiful, modern Hill Top Houses--a hostelry famed throughout the United States. Further northwest, overlooking the Potomac and Island Park, and separated from Magazine Hill by a deep ravine is Sunset Hill or Lover's Retreat. On this hill may be seen old rifle pits and breastworks of the Civil

War as well as a view of the Potomac and mountains well worth the toil of ascent to obtain. Opposite here in the Potomac is Island Park--a beautiful natural park, west from Harper's Ferry less than half a mile along the railroad and owned by the B.& O. Going on more directly west along the bluff, we reach Bolivar Heights, rich in war history, and about two miles west from Harper's Ferry. From the loftily heads of those heights views are afforded which for sublime magnificence, have been pronounced second to none in the world. About one mile west from the B.& 0. station at Harper's Ferry is the little town of Bolivar, which takes its name from Bolivar Heights, bounding it on the west. Leaving Bolivar Heights when in sight of the beautiful Shenandoah River and advancing eastward we pass the Lutheran Fairview cemetery, on the west of Boliver, then St. Peter's Catholic cemetery, then Circus Hill, now under cultivation and the property of Storer College. Next we reach Camp Hill, commanding a view of the

Shenandoah, Loudoun Heights, Herr's Island, the famous Gap, South Mountains and Maryland Heights, one of the finest views to be found in any part of the world. On this favored and historic spot stands Storer College, founded under the auspices of the Free Baptists in 1867 for the education and training of colored youth. The school was especially favored of heaven in securing the location. Storer's main buildings, Anthony Memorial Hall, Myrtle Hall and Lincoln Hall, stand right on the crown of Camp Hill. Here, too, is John Brown's Fort. This institution since its founding in 1867 has done splendid work for the education, training and uplift of the race and the cultivation of a better feeling between the races. Passing further east we come to the famous Lockwood House, standing on the eastern comb of Camp Hill. Lockwood House, once a chief government building, used by the superintendent of the arsenal and armory works at Harper's Ferry, and now Storer property through grant of the U. S.

government. Advancing eastward we next pass Harper's cemetery, where the remains of Harper lie. South of this Jefferson's Rock where Jefferson spent much time in study and wrote his notes on Virginia and declared the view from that rock worth a trip across the Atlantic. Looking southward we see the standing walls of the famous Herr's Mill: going on eastward we pass the standing walls of the old ruined Episcopal church, farther to the right is the staunch, new St. Peter's Catholic church. Next we pass the Old Stone dwelling house of Robt. Harper, built by Harper himself in 1780. On the way to the B.& O. station we pass John Brown's monument. Other places of special interest are numerous. Every spot about Harper's Ferry is very historic: indeed this is true of the whole of Jefferson County. It has the distinction of being the seat of the first settlements of the white man in the valley from the Potomac southward over 100 miles. From Harper's Ferry, northwest ten miles in Jefferson County, is Shepherdstown, the oldest town in the State and containing Shepherd's College, white; eight miles west is Charles Town, the county seat, containing the court house where John Brown and his men were tried and the spot of ground where he went through the climax of his heroic and victorious struggle for liberty. For the reasons named and others unnamed Harper's Ferry is distinguished as the best-known small town in the United States.

www.ingramcontent.com/pod-product-compliance
Lightning Source LLC
Chambersburg PA
CBHW020328170426
43200CB00006B/306